The Royal Court Theatre presents

# Porn Play

## By Sophia Chetin-Leuner

**Porn Play** was first performed at the Royal Court Jerwood Theatre Upstairs on Thursday 6 November 2025.

.

# Porn Play

By Sophia Chetin-Leuner

Cast (in alphabetical order)

Liam / Young Man / James / Sam **Will Close**
Student / Jasmine / Therapist / Doctor / Woman **Lizzy Connolly**
Dad / Old Man / Birkman **Asif Khan**
Ani **Ambika Mod**

Director **Josie Rourke**
Designer **Yimei Zhao**
Lighting Designer **Mark Henderson**
Movement Director **Wayne McGregor**
Sound Designer **Helen Skiera**
Dramaturg **Gillian Greer**
Casting Directors **Jessica Ronane CDG, Saffeya Shebli**
Assistant Director **Molly Stacey**
Production Manager **Marius Rønning**
Costume Supervisor **Ellen Rey de Castro**
Company Manager **Mica Taylor**
Stage Manager **Aime Neeme**
Deputy Stage Manager **Charlotte Padgham**
Lighting Supervisor **Lucinda Plummer**
Lighting Programmer **Lizzie Skellett**
Lead Producer **Charlie Bunker for Impossible Producing**
Executive Producer **Steven Atkinson**

Porn Play is a co-production with SISTER.
Sophia Chetin-Leuner is this year's recipient of The Clare McIntyre Bursary.

The Royal Court and Stage Management wish to thank the following for their help with this production:
Nica Burns CBE.

## Sophia Chetin-Leuner (Writer)

Theatre includes: **This Might Not Be It (Bush); Click & Collect (M6 Theatre Company); Ash (HighTide/Park); Save + Quit (VAULT/UK and Ireland Tour).**

Awards include: **BBC Writer's Room, Dalio Foundation Scholarship, Best of the Vault (Save + Quit), HighTide Academy Winner (Ash).**

## Will Close (Performer)

Theatre includes: **Dear England (National); Man Mountain, Bad Altitude, 1599, Great British Mysteries? (Soho); Mediocre White Male (Park Theatre); The Maze (Teatro Vivo); 1&Only, The Texas Tax Man (VAULT); Golem (Young Vic); Good People (English Theatre of Frankfurt).**

Television includes: **Silent Witness, Midsomer Murders, Death in Paradise, Dalgliesh, Buffering.**

Film includes: **Titan, Falling.**

Awards include: **Olivier Award for Best Actor in a Supporting Role (Dear England).**

## Lizzy Connolly (Performer)

Theatre includes: **Pygmalion (Old Vic); Cabaret (Lido de Paris); Assassins, Present Laughter (Chichester Festival); Sweet Charity (Donmar); Oklahoma! (BBC Proms On The Town (Regent's Park); The Twilight Zone (Almeida); Wild Party (The Other Palace); Once in a Lifetime (Young Vic); Indecent Proposal, Xanadu (Southwark Playhouse); Vanities (Trafalgar Studios); Dirty Rotten Scoundrels (Savoy); Mrs Henderson Presents (Royal Bath/ Noël Coward).**

Film includes: **The Festival.**

Television includes: **Dreaming Whilst Black S2, Criminal Record, Documentary, Now!, The Canterville Ghost, Call the Midwife, Plebs, The Windsors.**

**Asif Khan** (Performer)

...or the Royal Court: **A Kind of People.**

Theatre includes: **A Man for All Seasons (West End); Tartuffe (& Birmingham Rep), The Hypocrite (& Hull Truck) (RSC); Handbagged, Multitudes, When The Crows Visit (Kiln); Love, Bombs and Apples (Arcola/UK & USA tour); A Passage to India (Park Theatre); Hamlet, The Cherry Orchard (Theatre Royal Windsor); Great Expectations (Royal Exchange Theatre); Twelfth Night (National); Snookered (Bush); Mixed Up North (Bolton Octagon).**

Television includes: **Mr Bates vs The Post Office, Diana & I, Doctor Who, Spooks, Hapless, Going Postal.**

Film includes: **Love Type D, Hamlet.**

Radio includes: **The Archers.**

**Mark Henderson**
(Lighting Designer)

Theatre includes: **Girl From The North Country, Operation Mincemeat, Standing at the Sky's Edge, Chitty Chitty Bang Bang, The Iceman Cometh, The Judas Kiss, Copenhagen, Democracy, Hamlet, The Real Thing (& Broadway), The Sound of Music, Our House, Up for Grabs, Grease is the Word, West Side Story, Spend Spend Spend, Neville's Island, Follies, Passion, Enron, All My Sons, The Rise and Fall of Little Voice, Sweeney Todd, American Buffalo, The Bodyguard, Gypsy, Funny Girl, The Weir (West End); Racing Demon, Les Parent Terribles, Cat on a Hot Tin Roof (& Broadway), All My Sons, Mourning Becomes Electra, The History Boys, The Habit of Art, Dancing at Lughnasa, One Man Two Guvnors, The Hard Problem (National).**

Film includes: **The Tall Guy, Girl From The North Country.**

Architectural work includes: **Royal Court re-development, Madame Tussauds (London/Las Vegas/New York).**

Awards include: **Six Olivier Awards for Lighting Design.**

## Sir Wayne McGregor CBE
(Movement Director)

For the Royal Court: **Cleansed.**

Other theatre includes: **Dancing at Lughnasa, A Little Night Music, Antony & Cleopatra, Fram (National); Kirikou et Karaba (Casino De Paris); Closer, Sweet Charity (Donmar); You Never Can Tell, Much Ado About Nothing (Sheffield), Breakfast at Tiffany's, The Woman in White (& Broadway), Ring Around The Moon (West End); Aladdin, Cloaca (Old Vic); Hamlet (Royal Windsor).**

As artistic director of Company Wayne McGregor, dance includes: **On The Other Earth, Deepstaria, UniVerse: A Dark Crystal Odyssey, Living Archive: An AI Performance Experiment, Autobiography, +- Human, Tree of Codes, Atomos, FAR and Entity.**

Other dance works include: **MADDADDAM (& National Ballet of Canada), Untitled, 2023, The Dante Project, Yugen, Obsidian Tear, Woolf Works, Raven Girl, Carbon Life, Infra and Chroma (Royal Ballet), LORE (Teatro alla Scala); AfteRite (American Ballet Theatre); Genus, Alea Sands and L'Anatomie de la Sensation (Paris Opera Ballet); Sunyata (Bayerisches Staatsballett); Kairos (Ballett Zürich); Borderlands (San Francisco Ballet); EDEN|EDEN (Stuttgart Ballet); Outlier (New York City Ballet); Dyad 1929 (Australian Ballet); 2Human (English National Ballet); PreSentient (Rambert).**

Opera includes: **Jocasta's Line: Oedipus Rex/Antigone (Norwegian National Ballet & Opera), Orpheus and Eurydice, Salome, Noye's Flood (ENO), Dido and Aeneas (& Teatro alla Scala), Acis and Galatea, Sum (The Royal Opera House); Midsummer Marriage (Lyric Opera Chicago); The Marriage of Figaro, Orpheus and Eurydice, Hansel and Gretel (Scottish Opera).**

Concerts include: **ABBA Voyage (ABBA Arena Queen Elizabeth Olympic Park).**

Film includes: **Audrey, Mary Queen of Scots, Fantastic Beasts, Sing, The Leger of Tarzan, Harry Potter and the Goblet of Fire.**

Video work includes: **Torus for SHOWStud Winged Bull in the Elephant Case, Atomo: Lotus Flower (Radiohead), Wide Open (The Chemical Brothers).**

In 2024, His Majesty King Charles III appointed Wayne McGregor a Knighthood in the 2024 Birthday Honours List. He is artistic director of Studio Wayne McGregor, Resident Choreographer at The Royal Ballet and the current Artistic Director of Dance for La Biennale di Venezia.

## Ambika Mod (Performer)

Theatre includes: **Every Brilliant Thing, White Rabbit Red Rabbit (@ Soho Place).**

Television includes: **One Day, This is Going to Hurt, The Stolen Girl, I Hate Suzie.**

Awards include: **Royal Television Society Award for Best Supporting Actress (This Is Going to Hurt), Broadcast Press Guild Award for Best Actress (This Is Going to Hurt), Rose d'Or Emerging Talent Award (One Day), BAFTA Breakthrough, Forbes' 30 Under 30 in Europe, Time100 NEXT, Sunday Times Young Power List.**

## ...ime Neeme (Stage Manager)

or the Royal Court: **Scenes from a Repatriation, Gunter (& Dirty Hare), Bullring Techno Makeout Jamz (& Tour).**

Other theatre includes: **Bellringers, An Interrogation (Hampstead); Skye: A Thriller, Nation (Edinburgh Fringe); Hungry, Black Love, May Queen, Really Big and Really Loud, Parakeet (Roundabout).**

## Charlotte Padgham
(Deputy Stage Manager)

For the Royal Court: **Blue Mist, all of it (2023), Baghdaddy, Living Archive, For Black Boys Who Have Considered Suicide When The Hue Gets Too Heavy [job share], Rare Earth Mettle, Living Newspaper, all of it (2020), Midnight Movie, Cyprus Avenue JTD, ear for eye, Girls & Boys, a profoundly affectionate, passionate devotion to someone (-noun), hang, Posh (& West End), truth and reconciliation, Catch, On Insomnia and Midnight, The Winterling, My Name is Rachel Corrie (& West End), Fireface, The Force of Change, Dublin Carol.**

Other theatre includes: **Romans, Chimerica (& West End), Game (Almeida); Girl in the Machine, Life of Galileo (Young Vic); The Dream of a Ridiculous Man, The Dry House (Marylebone); Hamlet, King Lear (Globe); Complicit, Speed-the-Plow, All About My Mother, The Entertainer (Old Vic); Aristocrats, Appropriate, Fathers and Sons (Donmar); The Invisible Hand, The House That Will Not Stand, Red Velvet (& NY), The Bomb: a partial history, The Riots, Tactical Questioning, Greta Garbo Came to Donegal (Kiln); Shopping and F\*\*\*ing, Herons, Tipping the Velvet (Lyric Hammersmith); nut (National); Great Expectations, Onassis, Kurt & Sid (West End); Nocturnal, Medea Medea (Gate); Us and Them, Fragile Land (Hampstead); Bronte, A Passage to India (UK tour and Brooklyn Academy of Music); Gone to Earth, Madame Bovary, The Clearing, The Magic Toyshop, Mill on the Floss (UK & China tour and The Kennedy Center).**

## Ellen Rey de Castro
(Costume Supervisor)

For the Royal Court: **Scenes from a Repatriation.**

Other theatre includes: **The Jungle Book (Theatre By The Lake); Miss Myrtle's Garden (Bush Theatre) and The Hunger Games (Troubadour Canary Wharf).**

Dance includes: **Sleeping Beauty (Royal Ballet).**

Opera includes: **Lady Macbeth of Mtsensk, Simon Boccanegra (Royal Opera House).**

## Jessica Ronane CDG
(Casting Director)

Theatre includes: **The Real Thing, Pygmalion, The Dumb Waiter, Camp Siegfried, Faith Healer, Lungs, A Very Expensive Poison, Present Laughter, All My Sons (Old Vic); Stranger Things: The First Shadow, Long Day's Journey into Night, The Lehman Trilogy, The Glass Menagerie, A Mirror (& Almeida), People, Places and Things (West End); Grace Pervades (Theatre Royal Bath); The Little Foxes (Young Vic); The Spy Who Came In From the Cold, The Caretaker (Chichester Festival); Ulster American (Riverside Studios); Every Brilliant Thing (@ Soho Place); The Lady From The Sea (Bridge).**

Television includes: **True Detective: Night Country, The Amazing Mr Blunden.**

Film includes: **After The Hunt, The Woman in Cabin 10, Queer, Mickey 17, Good Grief, Emma, The Kid Who Would Be King.**

## Josie Rourke (Director)

For the Royal Court:
**Crazyblackmuthfuckin'self, Loyal Women, The Herd, Children's Day.**

Other theatre includes: **Dancing at Lughnasa, Men Should Weep (National); Lemons Lemons Lemons Lemons Lemons, As You Like It, Much Ado About Nothing (West End); Measure for Measure, Saint Joan, Les Liaisons Dangereuses (& Broadway), The Vote, Privacy (& Public Theater, NYC), City of Angels (& West End), Coriolanus, The Weir (& West End), Berenice, The Physicists, The Recruiting Officer, The Cryptogram, Frame 312, The Wrong Side of the Rainbow (Donmar); The Machine (Manchester International Festival); Sixty-Six Books, ...like a fishbone..., If There Is I Haven't Found it Yet, Apologia, 2,000 Feet Away, Tinderbox, How To Curse (Bush); Here (Riverside Studios); The Taming of the Shrew, Twelfth Night (Chicago Shakespeare Theater); The Life and Death of King John, Believe What You Will (RSC); The Long and the Short and the Tall (Lyceum, Sheffield); Much Ado About Nothing, The Unthinkable, World Music, Kick for Touch (Crucible, Sheffield); My Dad's a Birdman (Young Vic); The Vagina Monologues (UK Tour); Romeo and Juliet (Liverpool Playhouse).**

Television includes: **The Vote, Talking Heads.**

Film includes: **Mary Queen of Scots.**

**Josie was the Resident Assistant Director at the Donmar Warehouse, the Trainee Associate Director of The Royal Court Theatre, Associate Director of Sheffield Theatres, the Artistic Director of The Bush Theatre and of The Donmar Warehouse.**

## Helen Skiera (Sound Designer)

For the Royal Court: **Instructions For Correct Assembly, Bodies.**

Other theatre includes: **Juniper Blood (Donmar); Toto Kerblammo! (Unicorn); Peanut Butter and Blueberries (Kiln); F\*\*ked Up Bedtime Stories Series 2 (ETT); Cinderella, Red Riding Hood (Stratford East); Mind Mangler: Member of the Tragic Circle (& West End), Not: The Lovely Bones (& Birmingham REP), Lady Chatterly's Lover (UK Tour); The Long Song (Chichester Festival); A Christmas Carol (Bristol Old Vic); Out of Water (Orange Tree); Silence (Mercury); Here I Belong (Pentabus); This Is Not For You (Graeae); Imber: You Walk Through, Betrayal, Echo's End, The Magna Carta Plays (Salisbury Playhouse).**

As associate sound designer, theatre includes includes: **Lander 23, Viola's Room (Punchdrunk); The Encounter (Complicité); East is East (Birmingham REP & Chichester Festival ); Cat on a Hot Tin Roof (& Young Vic), Touching The Void (West End); Barbershop Chronicles (National).**

Radio includes: **The Dark Is Rising.**

## Molly Stacey (Assistant Director)

As staff director, theatre includes: **The Estate (National).**

As associate director, theatre includes: **The Weir, People, Places and Things, Why Am I So Single?, A Mirror (& Almeida) (West End), The Shark is Broken (UK Tour); and Babies the Musical (Other Palace).**

As director, theatre includes: **Like a Rat (Camden People's); John Tothill: The Last Living Libertine (& Soho Theatre), Pillow Talk (& Tour), Chelsea Birkby: This is Life, Cheeky Cheeky, Will Owen: Like Nobody's Watching (& Soho Theatre), Sarah Roberts: Silkworm (& Soho Theatre) (Edinburgh Fringe); Jinkies! (Camden Fringe).**

## Yimei Zhao (Designer)

Theatre includes: **The Society For New Cuisine (Omnibus); Before After (Southwark Playhouse); Dare You Say Please (King's Head).**

As associate designer, theatre includes: **The Hot Wing King (National); Bengal Tiger at the Baghdad Zoo (Young Vic); King Troll (New Diorama).**

Dance includes: **THE HEAT (Sadler's Wells/ The Lowry/ South East Dance).**

Film includes: **Men Without Women.**

Awards Include: **Linbury Prize for Stage Design.**

# THE ROYAL COURT THEATRE

**The Royal Court Theatre is the writers' theatre. It is a leading force in world theatre for cultivating and supporting writers – undiscovered, emerging and established.**

Since 1956, we have commissioned and produced hundreds of writers, from John Osborne to Mohamed-Zain Dada. Royal Court plays from every decade are now performed on stages and taught in classrooms and universities across the globe.

Through the writers, the Royal Court is at the forefront of creating restless, alert, provocative theatre about now. We open our doors to the unheard voices and free thinkers that, through their writing, change our way of seeing.

We strive to create an environment in which differing voices and opinions can co-exist. In current times, it is becoming increasingly difficult for writers to write what they want or need to write without fear, and we will do everything we can to rise above a narrowing of viewpoints. Through all our work, we strive to inspire audiences and influence future writers with radical thinking and provocative discussion.

ROYAL COURT

X royalcourt  f royalcourttheatre

ARTS COUNCIL ENGLAND

Supported using public funding by

# ROYAL COURT SUPPORTERS

Our incredible community of supporters makes it possible for us to achieve our mission of nurturing and platforming writers at every stage of their careers. Our supporters are part of our essential fabric – they help to give us the freedom to take bigger and bolder risks in our work, develop and empower new voices, and create world-class theatre that challenges and disrupts the theatre ecology.

To all our supporters, thank you. You help us to write the future.

**PUBLIC FUNDING**

Supported using public funding by
**ARTS COUNCIL
ENGLAND**

**CORPORATE SPONSORS & SUPPORTERS**
Aqua Financial Ltd
Bloomberg Philanthropies
Cadogan
Character 7
Concord Theatricals
Edwardian Hotels, London
Nick Hern Books
Phone Locker
Riverstone Living
Sloane Stanley
Sustainable Wine Solutions
Walpole

**STS
TER**

**TRUSTS & FOUNDATIONS**
Backstage Trust
Bruce Wake Charitable Trust
Chalk Cliff Trust
Clare McIntyre's Bursary
Cockayne - Grants for the Arts
The Common Humanity Arts Trust
Cowley Charitable Foundation
David Laing Foundation
The Davidson PlayGC Bursary
The Dominic Webber Trust - Core Values
The Fenton Arts Trust
Foyle Foundation
Genesis Foundation
The Golsoncott Foundation
Jerwood Foundation
John Thaw Foundation
The Katie Bradford Arts Trust
The Lynne Gagliano Writers' Award
The Marlow Trust
Martin Bowley Charitable Trust
Molecule Theatre Ltd
The Noël Coward Foundation
Old Possum's Practical Trust
Richard Radcliffe Charitable Trust
The Royal Borough of Kensington & Chelsea Arts Grant
Rose Foundation
The Sigrid Rausing Trust
The Thistle Trust
The Thompson Family Charitable Trust
The T.S. Eliot Foundation
Unity Theatre Trust
Y.A.C.K F.O

# INDIVIDUAL SUPPORTERS

### Artistic Director's Circle

Eric Abraham
Jeremy & Becky Broome
Clyde Cooper
Debbie De Girolamo &
Ben Babcock
Dominique & Neal Gandhi
Lydia & Manfred Gorvy
David & Jean Grier
Charles Holloway OBE
Linda Keenan
Brian and Dayna Lee
Andrew Rodger and Ariana
Neumann
Jack Thorne & Rachel Mason
Sandra Treagus for
ATA Assoc. LTD
Sally Whitehill & Mark Gordon
Anonymous

### Writers' Circle

Chris & Alison Cabot
Cas Donald
Robyn Durie
The Hon P N Gibson's Charity
Trust
Kater Gordon
Ellie & Roger Guy
Melanie J. Johnson
Nicola Kerr
Héloïse and Duncan
Matthews KC
Emma O'Donoghue
Clare Parsons & Tony Langham
Maureen & Tony Wheeler
Anonymous

### Directors' Circle

Piers Butler
Fiona Clements
Professor John Collinge
Julian & Ana Garel-Jones
Carol Hall
Dr Timothy Hyde
Elizabeth O'Connor & Adam
Bandeen
Rajeev Philip

### Platinum Circle

Moira Andreae
Banga family
Beverley Buckingham
Katie Bullivant
Anthony Burton CBE
Matthew Dean
Lucy & Spencer De Grey
Emily Fletcher
The Edwin Fox Foundation
Beverley Gee
Madeleine Hodgkin
Kate Howe
Roderick & Elizabeth Jack
Susanne Kapoor
David P Kaskel & Christopher
A Teano
Peter & Maria Kellner
Frances Lynn
Robert Ledger & Sally
Moulsdale
Mrs Janet Martin
Andrew McIver
Barbara Minto
Brian and Meredith Niles
Timothy Prager
Corinne Rooney
Sir Paul & Lady Ruddock
Sir William & Lady Russell
Anita Scott
Bhags Sharma
Dr Wendy Sigle
Rita Skinner
SolerCapital
James and Victoria Tanner
Mrs Caroline Thomas
Yannis Vasatis
Ian, Victoria and Lucinda
Watson
Sir Robert & Lady Wilson

With thanks to our Silver and
Gold Supporters, and our
Friends and Good Friends,
whose support we greatly
appreciate.

With special thanks to our
Production Circle Supporters
Natasha Cheung
Clyde Cooper
Ana & Julian Garel-Jones
Steve & Lorraine Groves
Melanie J. Johnson
Nicola Kerr

# Become a Member of our Supporters Circle

Our community of supporters is essential to the future and success of the Royal Court.

Thanks to their generosity, we can take bigger and bolder risks in our work and remain the leading force in world theatre for supporting writers.

## From £250 a year our Supporters' Circle receive:

- Priority Booking and access to sold-out shows
- Early access to £15 Mondays
- Complimentary tickets and playtexts
- Invitations to Supporters' Receptions
- Press Night parties and Season Launch events
- Unique insight opportunities such as
- Script Meetings, Set Tours and more

## Join Today

**Speak to our Box Office team to find out more about our Supporters' Circle levels, or visit royalcourttheatre.com/support-donate/.**

The English Stage Company at the Royal Court Theatre is a registered charity (No. 231242)

# PORN PLAY

Sophia Chetin-Leuner

Who overcomes by force, hath overcome but half his foe.

*John Milton,* Paradise Lost


All paradises are defined by who is not there,
by the people who are not allowed in.

*Toni Morrison*

## Acknowledgements

Thank you to everyone who was open to sharing with me.
Thank you also to the many people who believed in and helped
shape this play, especially Josie Rourke and Gill Greer.

*S.C-L.*

## Characters

ANI, *thirty, female*
DAD / OLD MAN / BIRKMAN, *various ages, male*
STUDENT / JASMINE / DOCTOR / WOMAN, *various ages,*
    *female*
LIAM / JAMES / SAM, *mid twenties–mid thirties, male*

## Notes

There is violent sexual imagery, including descriptions of abuse and rape, referenced throughout.

There is frequent reference and depiction of addiction.

A dash ( – ) indicates an interrupted thought or unfinished sentence.

An ellipses (…) suggests a loaded pause.

## A Note on the Design

For Ani, her imaginative, private space – her paradise – is porn. It's something she can escape to alone and uninterrupted. The real world is an intrusion into her private paradise.

One of the realisations throughout the play – which can be visual – is that Ani can't stay in her imaginative, pornographic paradise forever. She has to engage with the real, three-dimensional world. The outside world, shame and the extent of her addiction, creep in and soil her paradise.

*This text went to press before the end of rehearsals and so may differ slightly from the play as performed.*

## Prologue

*A* WOMAN *stands on the stage. She stands like she could be a child but her body is a woman's.*

*She seems really content, happy, completely unaware of the audience.*

*She spots something light and reflective – a mirror, a pond, a screen. She has to get on-all fours to look at it properly. She sees her reflection. She thinks she's incredibly beautiful. It delights her.*

*She reaches out to touch herself but can't. She tries again.*

*She leans her face down, holding her hair back so she can kiss herself.*

*She does.*

*She sticks her tongue out and licks herself.*

*She arches her back and licks it again.*

*She looks up at the audience to check if they're enjoying it.*

## One

*An event room.*

ANI *stands alone. An* OLD MAN *approaches her and taps his glass rhythmically.*

OLD MAN. Excuse me, can you top me up? I don't know where you are all hiding away. I can't find you anywhere.

ANI. What?

OLD MAN. I've *guzzled* this glass down –

ANI. Oh, no, sorry – I'm – I'm not a waiter – I'm – I – this is for me.

OLD MAN. What's that?

ANI (*louder*). I am the recipient of the –

*A* WOMAN, *older than* ANI, *glides towards her.*

WOMAN. Ani. Congratulations!

*She kisses her on the cheek.*

I see you've met Giles. He loved your book.

OLD MAN. Who?

WOMAN. Giles, this is Ani Sandhu. SHE WON THE AWARD.

OLD MAN. You? You're very young.

WOMAN. Isn't she? The youngest woman ever –

ANI. Person. Thank you.

WOMAN. You look gorgeous as well, darling! Doesn't she? Hardly seems fair!

*They laugh.*

OLD MAN. Sandhu is an interesting name, where's that from?

ANI. Will you excuse me I –

ANI *turns away and collides with* SAM.

Sorry!

SAM. No, that was my bad. Sorry.

WOMAN. Darling, did you know Lensk is here?

OLD MAN. Lensk is here!

*They leave.*

SAM *offers a hand to shake.*

SAM. I'm Sam. Sam Lister. Big fan. Loved the book. Well deserved. Really well deserved.

ANI. Thank you. Are you a – sorry – what brings you here?

SAM. I'm about to start my masters. Under Birkman.

ANI. Oh great. He's great. You'll have a great time –

OLD MAN. Excuse me, can you top me up?

ANI. Have you seen him actually? I don't want to start without him –

SAM. Yeah it's going really well actually. I'm just trying to figure out the right angle

ANI. Sure. Well that will all reveal itself with –

(*Off his look.*) What?

SAM. Look at you, are you feeling a bit overwhelmed?

*He touches her arm.* ANI *looks at it.*

ANI. I'm fine.

SAM. It's an insane achievement. Congratulations, seriously well deserved.

ANI. Thank you.

SAM. You should be proud.

ANI. I am.

SAM. I actually went to your lecture series at the UFV when I was doing my A Levels.

ANI. Oh you saw those did you? That's kind. Thanks.

SAM. I'm a very big fan. Your work on Lacan has been so inspirational to my own –

ANI. I'm honoured. Good luck with it all. I'm just going to prep my –

SAM. Sorry if this is – but would you be down for getting a coffee sometime?

ANI. Uhmm – I …

SAM. Maybe I could get your number?

ANI. Why don't you email me.

SAM. Bit easier if I had your –

ANI. Birkman will give you my email.

SAM. Why –

ANI. Do you know if he's here yet?

SAM. Who?

ANI. Birkman!

SAM. Um yeah I think I saw him –

> WOMAN *and* OLD MAN *reappear suddenly.*

WOMAN. Wait! Tell us what's next!

SAM. I'll email you –

> *He leaves.*

OLD MAN. It's a good chunk of money – you can take three years off to write and live like a queen.

ANI. I think I'll stay teaching, I like teaching.

WOMAN. God why?!

OLD MAN. What's the second book?

ANI. I actually don't know yet –

WOMAN. Nor do you need to! The world is your oyster!

ANI. Have you seen Birkman?

WOMAN. No. I don't know how you do it – spend all your time in the head of that vile old man Milton. But yes she's bloody brilliant. You'll see – no wait. You have seen her speak before! Yes. In Vienna. Do you remember? The Civil War conference?

OLD MAN. Oh, so I did.

ANI. Clearly left an impression.

OLD MAN. Was that the one with all the African countries –

ANI. Okay bye!

WOMAN. No no no. You have to go get your award now! Give your little thank-yous.

ANI. I just need to –

OLD MAN. I look forward to seeing you speak, my dear.

WOMAN. Please – for after.

*She ushers* ANI *up.*

It is my absolute *pleasure* to present this award – from the Royal Fellowship Society Foundation Trust – to the brilliant, the luminous, the gifted… Anisha Sandhu!

*She hands the award to* ANI. *Maybe it's the pie from the next scene.*

*Blackout.*

## Two

*Two weeks earlier.* ANI *and her boyfriend* LIAM *sit opposite each other at a café. They have a slice of apple pie between them.*

LIAM. We'll do something proper this weekend.

ANI. I love this. Thank you.

LIAM. Here's to you! Congratulations!

Is there going to be a thing? Do you have to do a speech?

ANI. Yeah! There's going to be a ceremony thing in a few weeks.

LIAM. Exciting. Can't wait.

*They cheers forks and go to dig in.*

ANI. It could be you next time.

LIAM (*lowering his fork*). Don't say that.

ANI. Sorry, I – I just think it could be. Your new draft is great –

LIAM. Let's enjoy *your* success, yeah? It's well deserved.

*They smile at each other. Maybe share a kiss.*

Plus the competition for Modernism is insane.

*ANI raises her eyebrows.*

ANI. What does that mean?

LIAM. Nothing. Sorry. I'm so proud of you. Eat!

*ANI takes a bite of pie.*

Is it good?

ANI. Delicious. Have some.

*She offers him her fork. He dodges it.*

What's wrong?

LIAM (*pulling an icky face*)....Apple.

ANI. Why didn't you say?

LIAM. I wanted you to pick!

ANI. Thanks?

*She takes another bite.*

*It's a bit awkward.*

What?

LIAM. I want to voice a concern.

*LIAM shifts in his seat.*

ANI. Go on…

LIAM. I have to pretend my keys are getting jammed in the door so you have time to shut your fucking laptop!

ANI. No you don't.

LIAM. Last night the light from your phone woke me up! Again!

ANI. What? Where is this –
Is this about my award?

LIAM. No! No.
It's not! It's – I'm worried about you.
You don't seem interested in me any more.

ANI. Okay. Shall we try incorporating it in again? You used to like it.

LIAM. Yeah but – it used to be fun when it it was – but the stuff you watch is so –

ANI. Oh so this is about *what* I watch?

LIAM. Yes – no –

ANI (*mimicking*). Yes – no – oh talking about vaginas is so stressful!

LIAM. I will not go down on you while you watch that shit! Don't you feel bad? I feel a lot of shame after I beat one out –

ANI. Don't say beat one out.

*They laugh.*

It's over half the internet – you can't –

LIAM. Then why are you a vegetarian?

…

ANI. You just have to engage with it in ethical ways.

LIAM. You don't do that.

ANI. Yes I do!

LIAM. You don't pay for your porn!

ANI. Yes I do! Just because I don't tell you everything doesn't mean –

LIAM. What service do you subscribe to?

ANI *falters.*

ANI. The Pornhub one.

LIAM. That's not true.

ANI. You should try some of this before I finish it. It's really good. You can't taste it –

…

Okay, not that I need to explain this to you – but I like watching. It helps me unwind. To masturbate after a long day. It's like my glass of wine.

LIAM. Four glasses of wine.

ANI. Without the associated risks of cancer!

LIAM. Why don't you just – not? Or just. Wake me up? If you're in need of release? I'm right here. I could do that.

ANI *laughs.*

What? I can't do that?

ANI. It's not the same. It requires much more… work.

LIAM *throws his hands up in exasperation.* ANI *catches one.*

Hey – hey – can we not make this about your ego, please? I'm sure you understand that sometimes you just want to do it by yourself…

*He doesn't. She rolls her eyes.*

LIAM. I'm just trying to understand why you like this stuff. It's so – not what you are like. Not what you like.

ANI. Exactly – it's all fake.

LIAM. What is?

ANI. The stuff on screen.

LIAM. How can *that* be fake? The hands over the face. It's –

*He's genuinely disgusted.*

It's scary.

ANI. Look, that kind of thing is very common for women.

LIAM. Is it?

ANI. Women are twice as likely to search for violent porn than men.

LIAM. What?

ANI. I'll send you the study.

*She takes another bite of pie.* LIAM *is a bit at a loss.*

LIAM. Why?

ANI. I don't know. Unpicking human desire is so stupid. No one knows why they like the things they like.

LIAM. That is such shit. You unpick things for a living!

ANI. Come on. I'm not calling you a racist for loving 'latina natural boobs'! I'm not questioning why men love to watch handjob videos. Really close-up handjob videos.

LIAM *is shy.*

LIAM. Maybe they just get so used to being treated like shit they start to search it out. Like a Pavlovian dog thing.

ANI. Let's pause on the comparing women to dogs thing, yeah, Liam?

LIAM. Sorry.
And like don't women – straight women – watch gay porn? Like two men?

ANI. Exactly. It's porn. It's not representative – it's not real!

LIAM (*not convinced*). Yeah.

ANI (*joking*). Maybe women just have secret dangerous parts of us that you can't even begin to understand.

LIAM (*sighing*). Yeah. Probably.
Harry didn't even think women could get addicted to porn.

ANI. Addicted?

LIAM. Yeah he said that he didn't think that women had that dirty-pervert sex drive that men have.

ANI. I'm so pleased you got Harry to weigh in on this.

LIAM. Well, he had some interesting things to say.

ANI. Like expressing surprise that women have sex drives?

LIAM. No, but like he just thought that they have better – like – boundaries with sex stuff. Or they don't have that like rabid urge that men do. Or they do but they can turn it off.

ANI. I don't know whether you are doing like a 'rape is part of nature' thing or a 'teenage boy with blue balls' thing – but either way can you stop.

LIAM. I'm just trying to understand, Ani.

ANI *laughs.*

Stop laughing. I am finding it – this –

ANI. Threatening? You don't like your 'woman' to have desires outside of you.

LIAM. No. That's not it and you know it. Don't start throwing second wave at me and let me try to. Articulate. Myself. Can't you see how upset I am – don't you want to acknowledge my feelings? Meet me halfway?

ANI. With what?

LIAM. Like, agreeing to cut down a bit?

ANI. I can't believe we are here, bargaining over my sexuality.

LIAM. That is not what this is –

ANI. Isn't it though? Or is that just pseudotherapy language that men now use to pull the same controlling shit?

LIAM *puts his head in his hands.*

LIAM. I am a person in this relationship too.

ANI. I actually don't believe this. *You* watch it. *You* get to do it.

LIAM. Not as much –

ANI. Why can't I watch porn in the same way men do? I bet there are tons of men you know who watch as much – if not more – than me? Fucking Harry can fucking do one. What, he just hides it better? Like that's any healthier?

LIAM. It's not the same!

ANI. How? How is it not?

LIAM (*like a child*). Because it's not! It's not the same!

*She looks at him with disgust.*

ANI. What is going on with you?

*He looks around, self-conscious.*

Can you hear yourself? I'm a bit shocked, to be honest. Why is my boyfriend ambushing me in a public place telling me that the thing I enjoy – in *private* – the thing that helps me relax, to access pleasure, the thing that taught me to orgasm –

LIAM. Ani – shhh –

ANI. No I'm not going to shh! This whole conversation is insane and says more about you really – that you're a prude. Or that you've got some untapped part of your sexuality that you're deeply ashamed of. What? Do you want to fuck a pig or something? You don't know why you love little braided ponytails so much? Or you're worried you're gay because of all those fucking HANDJOB videos?!

LIAM. Can you calm down please?

*She calms.*

ANI. I'm stressed right now. This – award – it's great but it brings with it a lot of pressure. I don't know what the second book is going to be about –

LIAM. I know.

ANI. And I need to go see my dad. I – it's coming up –

LIAM. What? Oh.

ANI. Yeah. There's a lot going on.

LIAM. I know, I'm sorry.

ANI. Why are you making me feel like something is wrong with me?

*He looks at her with empathy. He takes her hand.*

LIAM. I'm sorry.

…

ANI. Maybe you should think about what it is about it that bothers you so much?

LIAM. I'll… yeah I'll think about it.

ANI. Maybe take it to therapy.

LIAM. I will.

ANI. I don't know if it's about the award or what but – this is not okay.

LIAM. I know it's not.

ANI. Is it about the award?

…

LIAM. Maybe, yeah.

ANI. I didn't think you were like that.

LIAM. I'm not. I promise. I love you.

*Maybe he kisses her hand.*

I'm so sorry.

*She looks at him. Lets go of his hand and picks up her fork.*

ANI. Have a bit of pie.

LIAM. I'm okay.

ANI. You should try it.

LIAM. I don't want any.

ANI. Just have a little taste, Liam.

LIAM. Finish it.

ANI. It's really good.

LIAM. (*flipping out*). I don't want any pie, Ani!

*She puts the folk down.*

*They survey each other.*

…

*He relents, taking a bite of the pie. He chews.*

You're right. This is good pie.

*He eats more.* ANI *looks at him, disgusted.*

ANI. I don't think I'm happy with you.

LIAM. What?

ANI. I think we should break up.

**Three**

*Ani's childhood bedroom.*

ANI – *laptop open – lies in bed. She's working. She sighs, bored, and looks around.*

*She bends down and pulls a box out from under her bed.*

*A smile emerges on her face – the first time we've seen a proper smile from her.*

*She selects a vibrator and grins. Maybe even giggles.*

*She searches for something to watch on her laptop.*

*She seems to relax as she starts masturbating.*

*Bzzzz Bzzzzz –*

DAD (*offstage*). Ani, can you give me a hand with your stuff?

*Suddenly a swift knock and her* DAD *walks in.*

ANI *slams her laptop shut and shoves the box under her bed, it doesn't quite slide under and remains half poking out.*

ANI. Dad oh my god you can't just walk in like that, have you ever heard of knocking?

DAD. I did knock.

ANI. No you didn't!

DAD. Ani, I did knock. Can you please find time to move some of these boxes today?

ANI. Yes.

DAD. Well, you've been saying that –

ANI. Yes I know I'll do it okay? I'll do it today!

*He looks at her in bed.*

DAD. Before this evening please.

*He hovers.*

ANI. What?

DAD. It's just a lot of stuff for – for three weeks.

ANI *is exasperated.*

ANI. I mean if it's a problem I can always stay with Jasmine –

DAD. Don't be stupid.

ANI. I wanted to get all my stuff from Liam's so there's no back and forth –

DAD. Mm.

*He opens one of the boxes by her door.*

ANI. You don't have to do that –

DAD *holds up a stack of books.*

DAD. Back on the shelf or?

ANI. Leave it, I'll do it.

DAD. Bins go out tonight so –

DAD *goes to unpack another box.* ANI *tenses as he walks past her sex toy box.*

I'm just heading out to the school plot. The tulips are giving us some trouble. I can give you a lift to the station if you like.

ANI. When?

DAD. In five.

ANI. Can't you wait half an hour? I'm not ready.

DAD. No I can't wait, no, I'm going to work. You heard of it?

*She makes no move to get up.* DAD *sighs and checks his watch.*

It's gone eleven. Come on, time to get out of bed. Don't you need to be practising or something?

ANI. It's fine. It's basically just an extract from my book and some thank yous so nothing crazy. And it's not for ages.

DAD. When is it?

ANI. Why, do you want to come?

DAD. If you want me to.

ANI *rolls her eyes.*

Still. Good to keep busy.

ANI. Yeah the famous professor is coming from America so it's kinda a big deal.

DAD. Right. Don't you have to be doing flat viewings or something? Where are you going to live?

ANI. Can't I just have some time to decompress? Jesus I'm not that bad, am I?

DAD. No. No. Of course not.

*He waits.* ANI *just blinks at him.*

Um. So. Are you –
Um
Are you okay?

ANI. What yeah I'm fine.

DAD. You're not… too sad about
About Liam?

*DAD sits on the edge of her bed awkwardly. The vibrator is under there. ANI tenses.*

ANI. Yeah. I am quite sad.

DAD. Nice man. Shame.

*DAD sighs, slaps his thighs, and reaches down to get the box at his feet.*

ANI. Wait –

*ANI bolts up to stop him but it's too late.*

*He stares down at the box of sex toys. He looks pale, disgusted.*

DAD. These are yours, are they?

*ANI nods.*

*She giggles, awkwardly.*

ANI. I guess this is why adult daughters don't stay with their dads.

*She reaches for the box.*

*He hesitates.*

Come on, Dad, I know it's not pleasant but we aren't Mormons.

*She yanks the box out of his grip.*

DAD.…Are you sure you're okay?

ANI. I'm fine.
Go away!

*He hovers.*

Dad!

DAD. Okay Okay! I'll knock louder next time.

## Four

*Ani's office at work. A knock.*

ANI. Yeah.

STUDENT. Hiya, do you have a sec?

ANI. Yes. Come in – sorry – you're in my second-year seminar right? Bex?

STUDENT. Yes!

ANI. Hi hi, come in, Bex, what can I help you with?

STUDENT. I just wanted to talk about your lecture this morning.

ANI. Course, come in, what can I – oh I love your shoes!

STUDENT. Thanks?

ANI. So cute. Where are they from?

STUDENT. Um. I think the – I actually don't remember, sorry.

ANI. That's okay. Come in.

STUDENT (*indicating the door*). Do you want it –

ANI. Leave it open, it gets so hot in here.

STUDENT. Okay.

ANI. So what's up?

STUDENT. Um. I was a bit upset after your lecture.

ANI. Oh no. Is everything okay?

STUDENT. You were talking about some upsetting things.

ANI. In the lecture?

STUDENT. Yes, and – and you didn't give us a trigger warning or anything.

ANI. I'm very sorry to upset you, Bex. It's never my intention to cause anyone discomfort or pain. Did you check the content warnings beforehand?

STUDENT. Uh – no.

ANI. Okay, I think – in future – that's maybe worth doing. I put content warnings on all my syllabi.

STUDENT. Oh. Okay. Sorry.

ANI. No need to be sorry.

   …

STUDENT. It's just.

ANI. Mm?

STUDENT. Um. You said the phrase 'rape is sexy'.

   …

ANI. That is not what I said.

STUDENT. It is.

*She gets out her phone.*

ANI. What are you –

STUDENT. I record the lectures. Listen back over them, helps me retain.

*She searches for the right time stamp and presses play –*
*ANI's voice comes out from her phone:*

*'Milton's patron's relative had recently been executed because he raped these young boys who were working for him and made them rape his wife. So Milton is basically glorifying his death in a way by making rape seem okay – seem sexy.'*

ANI. Right. Well. I'm obviously not saying that – in the context of the lecture – it's about the subversive nature of Milton's sexual language –

STUDENT. But the whole thing was about this girl getting kidnapped by Bacchus –

ANI. No, by Comus, *son* of Bacchus –

STUDENT. Right but –

ANI. – and how Milton is interested in these linguistic somersaults. I was not taking sexual assault lightly.

STUDENT. But you kept saying it was *sexy.*

ANI *goes to close the door, annoyed by the constant interruptions.*

Please can we leave it open?

ANI *looks shocked.*

ANI. Yes, of course.

STUDENT. It's really hot in here. You're right.

ANI *relaxes. Sort of.*

ANI. Bex, if you want to talk to a counsellor about why it may have upset you I am more than happy to email over details –

STUDENT. It's okay. I just wanted to let you know. You never know what people are going through.

ANI. No, you don't. That's why I put content warnings on the syllabus.

…

This feels like it could be a really exciting jumping-off point for your next essay. Have you thought about what your next one will be on?

STUDENT *shakes her head.*

Well, why don't you play around this? You could take a look at Gilbert and Gubar. And you can try Wittreich – W-I-T-T-R-E-I-C-H. He's got some good insights.

STUDENT. Will it get me a better mark?

ANI *goes to speak but stops herself.*

I didn't not understand it, if that's what you're thinking. I just don't buy it.

ANI *frowns in frustration.*

ANI. Okay.

STUDENT. I don't mean to offend you or your work. You must be very well respected – you won that thing. That's amazing. It's just – you sound good. I am convinced in the moment. But then I go home and try to write my essay and all I can see is that Eve is pretty and stupid.

ANI. Well – I obviously disagree with you there –

STUDENT. Milton wouldn't agree with anything you say though.

ANI. Well, Milton's not here.

STUDENT (*laughing*). Thank fuck.

ANI. Sorry, I just want to flag, I don't think you'd – careen – into one of your male professors' offices and start ranting and swearing at them like this, would you?

*The* STUDENT *looks shocked.*

STUDENT. Uh – I'm sorry.

*The* STUDENT *leans forward provocatively.*

I don't mean to be a naughty girl.

*The* STUDENT *returns to how she was sitting before.* ANI *blinks back into focus.*

I'm sorry. I don't mean to be disrespectful. I was just really excited for this course. Maybe naively. I'm just so sick of trying to bend over backwards to understand these men. Like. I don't know. I get death of the author and all that but. Did you know Milton beat the schoolboys he taught? That his first wife left their home in London because she couldn't – like – stand the noise of it?

ANI. I did.

STUDENT. So. Like. Why would you want to read him and analyse all these – these horrible men? These rapists? Right? They're rapists. I don't want to read anything from a rapist's brain. I don't really care if someone thinks it's good. And I guess I thought – I guess I'm stuck on why –

ANI. Is everything alright, Bex?

STUDENT. I think I just hate Milton, sorry.

ANI. That's okay, a lot of people do.
Why are you taking this module then?

STUDENT. I don't know. I guess I just wanted to take a course
with a female lecturer.

## Five

ANI *is in bed. The sound of the same Bzzz Bzzz – is she
masturbating again? No, it's* JASMINE, *in a state of half–
undress, brushing her teeth with an electric toothbrush.*

JASMINE. But if it's not matte it just gets on my teeth – see it's
everywhere.

*She shows* ANI *the lipstick on her teeth and toothbrush.* ANI
*murmurs in reply.*

JASMINE *disappears off stage and comes back without the
toothbrush.*

*She's taking her make-up off with a wipe. She throws it
casually to the side and climbs into bed next to* ANI.

EEEEE a sleepover it's been sooo long

*She snuggles* ANI.

ANI. I knowwww. Thanks for letting me crash. It won't be for
long – my dad is just being a bit –

JASMINE. Your dad –

ANI (*laughing*). Yeah –

JASMINE. I don't want you returning to the mausoleum for
sure. Stay here for as long as you want, baby.

*JASMINE squeezes her hand.*

Are you okay?

ANI. Yessss stopppp.

JASMINE. Did you miss him tonight?

ANI. Not really.

JASMINE. Do you not want to talk about it at alllll.

ANI. There's not much to say.

JASMINE. But whyyyy –

ANI. I don't know we just we – we wanted different things.

JASMINE. It's hard to believe Liam wouldn't just want
whatever you want.

*ANI shrugs out of* JASMINE*'s grip.*

ANI. Well! Guess I'm that impossible!

JASMINE. No no shut up.

*JASMINE whacks a pillow over* ANI.

*ANI screams and throws one back at* JASMINE.

*A specific movement shifts the energy.*

*They have a pillow fight with fake porn gasps, moans and
squeals. Maybe there's touching and rubbing.*

*Suddenly – the specific movement repeats, and we are back
in reality.*

*JASMINE leaps up and jumps on the bed excitedly.* ANI *gets
off the bed, a little awkward.*

Oh my god I forgot to tell you Ellie Palmer got herpes!

ANI. No?

JASMINE. Yeah.

ANI. From her fiance?

JASMINE. Yeah apparently he was sleeping with prostitutes!
She looked on his phone one day and he kept getting an
Uber to this one location and she thought he was having an
affair but she looked at the location and it was a brothel! In
Harrow! She had to get an HIV test and everything.

ANI. That's so sad.

JASMINE *scratches her arm…*

Maybe it'll make her a nicer person.

JASMINE *cackles and collapses on the bed next to* ANI.

JASMINE. You're terrible.
But also how weird 'cause I swear she got the jab with us?

ANI. It doesn't prevent herpes.

JASMINE. Oh does it not?

ANI. No just supposed to limit your risk of cervical cancer.

JASMINE *nods in knowing respect and cuddles* ANI *pointedly.*

JASMINE. You know my arm still gets itchy where they jabbed us?

ANI. Bullshit.

JASMINE. I swear look –

*She shows* ANI *her upper arm.*

ANI. You're making that up. Jasmine.

JASMINE. No I'm not!

ANI. What possible scientific explanation could you possibly have to a vaccine you got over ten years ago making your arm itch occasionally?

JASMINE (*mimicking*). What possible scientific explanation –

ANI *rolls over, turning away from* JASMINE.

ANI. Liam cheated on me.

JASMINE. What?

ANI. I don't want to talk about it any more but that's why I've been acting like such a bitch, okay?

JASMINE. Okay, of course. Don't worry. Oh my god.

*She strokes* ANI.

Ani, I'm so sorry. I love you.

*She spoons her.*

When you want to talk about it –

ANI. Thank you.

…

I think something is wrong with me.

JASMINE. Nothing's wrong with you.

ANI. I'm weird about sex.

JASMINE. We're all weird about sex.

ANI. You didn't get sent home from sleepovers –

JASMINE *sits up.*

JASMINE. Oh come on that was years ago.

ANI *shakes her head.*

So what? You were a little horny teenager, fuck the weird mums for making it weird.

ANI. You've never done anything like that.

JASMINE. No but I've got my own shit.

ANI *is like 'yeah right'.*

I do!
You know in Year 9 we had that substitute maths teacher Mr Franklin for like two terms?

ANI. Yeah.

JASMINE. He really liked me. 'Cause I was good at maths but also 'cause I was friendly and rolled my skirt up. He used to ask me to stay behind after and tell me I was worth way more than the girls I hung out with and when was I going to realise my full potential and that I was so special.

ANI. Jas –

JASMINE. Relax. He fondled me a bit but I just told Mrs Simmons and he was gone – I think to another school actually yikes but – it's so weird 'cause like I'm constantly seeking that feeling when I'm fucking. Like if someone wants me to cum all they really have to do is be like 'you're so special'. How fucked up is that? 'Cause if they do actually start to see me as special then it completely repulses me. Like I can't see them again.

ANI. Is that what happened with Jay?

JASMINE. Ugh yeah. But see? Everyone has a thing, don't stress.

ANI. Jas, I'm so sorry why didn't you tell me?

JASMINE. It's fine. You had a lot going on. And it's not as horrific as it sounds, honestly.

*She rolls over, her back to* ANI.

OOOF I am EXHAUSTED.

JASMINE *sits up again, concerned.*

But are you okay? We can talk about Liam being the biggest fucking cunt in the whole world if –

ANI. No no. It's fine. I'm tired too.

JASMINE. Well, if you're ready to talk about it tomorrow I'm here –

ANI. Thank you.

JASMINE. Is my make-up off properly ?

*She shoves her face in* ANI*'s.*

ANI. Yep.

JASMINE *smacks* ANI *on the bum and rolls over, facing away.*

JASMINE. Gotta do the skincare. We ain't getting any younger.

*She yawns and switches the light off.*

Are you sure you're alright?

ANI. Yeah.

JASMINE. I'm always here.

JASMINE *throws a drunk, sleepy hand on* ANI *at an awkward angle, back still turned to her.*

ANI. I know.

> ANI *strokes her hand for a while in the near dark.*

> What porn do you like?

JASMINE (*sleepily*). Lol. Ummm whatever is on the homepage? Why?

ANI. I watch horrible stuff.

> JASMINE *rolls back to face* ANI.

> Is that bad?

JASMINE. No, babe.

ANI. Isn't it bad to… women?

JASMINE. You're a woman.

ANI. But sometimes I'm the one doing it to the – the woman.

JASMINE. Maybe you're a dom!

ANI. Or maybe I'm just watching it.

JASMINE. That's fun.

ANI. Doesn't that make me just as bad as men?

JASMINE. Well, you're not actually doing it, so no.

ANI. I guess I'm worried that – that I want to do this stuff – or have it done to me – or that it's seeping into me and affecting the way I see women and the world and – and myself. Like I look at women on the street and the first thing I think about is how their bodies fold and –

> JASMINE *turns the light on again.*

JASMINE. Babe, what are we talking about here? Are you okay?

> ANI *doesn't know.*

> Are you still seeing that therapist lady?

ANI. Yeah

JASMINE. I think you're overthinking it babe. Truly. I'd say as long as it's not animals or kids, you're good. Maybe you can explore your sexuality a bit if you're thinking about women all the time. But it's not that deep. I promise. Just enjoy yourself.

ANI. Promise?

JASMINE. Promise. You are not the only one who thinks they're a big ol freak. If it makes you feel any better men always want to fuck the hole where my colostomy bag is.

ANI. Oh my god! No they don't!?

*The girls cackle.*

JASMINE. Men love holes.

*The girls continue to laugh. It all seems okay.*

ANI. Do you let them?

JASMINE. Not any more!

*Another surge of laughter. It dies down when* JASMINE *yawns.*

Babe, I have to get my six hours.

ANI. Yes of course. Sorry. Love you.

JASMINE. Night, love you.

*She switches the light off.*

It's all going to be okay.

*Soon, the sound of* JASMINE'*s heavy breathing.*

ANI *looks over at* JASMINE.

*She's fast asleep.*

ANI *tries to join her. She can't.*

*She reaches over to grab her phone that's charging on the bedside table.*

*She goes on a porn website, searches 'schoolgirls' and starts masturbating under the covers.*

*This drags out. She pauses when* JASMINE *rolls over or mutters something in her sleep. But then she resumes.*

*Her orgasm builds. She is trying to stay quiet.*

*Her motions get more rhythmic.*

ANI *can't stop now – she bucks under the covers, gasping – pure euphoria.*

*She finishes.*

*Some moments pass.*

JASMINE *slowly gets out of bed and heads towards the bathroom –*

ANI. Jas? What you doing?

JASMINE. Going to the bathroom.

ANI. Are – you okay?

JASMINE (*coldly*). Yeah.

## Six

ANI. Hello. Hi. Welcome to Introduction to Milton. It's good to see so many of you here. Milton is a hard sell, so I'm glad you're willing to give him a go. Maybe some of you did *Paradise Lost* at school. I think Book Two – the fall and rise of Satan – is on the syllabus. But today we're going to be looking at the best supporting character: Eve.

And we know Eve is taken from the rib of Adam. We know she's often painted in the Bible, Torah, Quran as a lesser and subservient person. We hopefully also know she is tempted by Satan to eat the apple and we know this causes the fall of mankind. We may *not* know that Milton writes that the shame of that almost makes her take her own life!

But we're getting ahead – Milton first introduces us to Eve in Book Four of *Paradise Lost*. He pays a sort of 'homage' to the myth of Narcissus when he describes how she 'wakes up' and is immediately drawn to this liquid plain of 'unmoved' water – I love that image – of still, smooth, untroubled water. She bends down to look at it. It seems to her 'another sky'. And then she suddenly sees this shape in it. This collection of shapes. And she is so – so taken with it that she keeps looking at it. Staring at it. Fascinated by it. And then the voice of God comes up behind her and tells her 'what thou seest, is thyself'…

And she can't quite believe it. Like, imagine not being able to recognise yourself. How hard that would be to get your head around – that the thing you're looking at is actually you. It's like when babies – or cats – look in the mirror and struggle with the fact that this other thing is moving at the same time as them. So when Eve is told that she's looking at herself she quite literally has a moment of self-reflection. Isn't that beautiful? It's okay come in, take a seat.

But the thing is – and here is when it gets really interesting, I think – is that the person, the collection of shapes, you are looking at is both you and not you. For one thing, it is in reverse – so not quite you. And for another it is separate from you. You can't touch it. If Eve puts her hand in the water to try and touch herself, she'll disappear. If you try to touch the screen… Phones down please.

*A shift.*

It's funny, when I got out of the shower today I was brushing my hair and looking in the mirror and I had a similar experience. I see the toilet behind me in the mirror – through the reflection – and it reminds me of one of the videos I was watching before I got up. A man wearing a knuckle duster forces a woman's head into the toilet bowl – into the water – and fucks her in the ass while she thrashes around for air. If she thrashes too much he punches her in her side. So I guess I had a sort of Eve moment. I looked at my reflection and I didn't recognise myself.

*A shift back.*

Phones down please.

**Seven**

*A bed. Post-sex.*

LIAM. How was that?

ANI. Good, yeah.

LIAM. I'm so happy to see you.

ANI. Me too.

LIAM. Do you want some water?

ANI. Yes please.

> LIAM *gets up and leaves.*
>
> ANI *stares after him. She scrolls on her phone. She looks at the door.*
>
> *She puts her phone down and crosses her arms.*
>
> *Looks at the bed sheets.*
>
> *She looks distressed. She wriggles in resistance.*
>
> *But she can't resist.*
>
> *She lunges for her phone and starts watching porn and masturbating. Her body relaxes.*
>
> LIAM *comes back in.*

LIAM. What are you doing?

ANI. Come join me. Please.

> *He climbs onto the bed. They start kissing.* ANI *peers at her phone screen.* LIAM *does too. He immediately pulls away –*

LIAM. Jesus.

ANI. What?

LIAM. That poor woman.

ANI. It's all fake.

LIAM. How can that be fake?
　　Come on, put it away. This is –

ANI. Let me just find this good one –

LIAM. Please just put it away.

*She puts her phone down. He looks at her.*

Are you okay?

ANI. Stop making me feel bad about it.

LIAM. I'm not –

ANI. Are you saying I don't feel bad?

LIAM. I'm not saying you're not feeling that. I'm sorry.
I don't mean to make you feel bad.
I'm worried. Our relationship was ruined cause of it.

ANI *scoffs.*

ANI. No it wasn't.

LIAM. I miss you.

*He nudges her with his head, kisses her arm.*

*She grabs her phone back.*

This is getting on my nerves now, Ani.

ANI. Just leave me alone.

LIAM. You're at my house! You can't just show up in the
middle of the night with no explanation –

ANI. (*laughing*) It was nine p.m.

LIAM. Oh you know what? You can fuck off – you can leave –
I don't –

ANI *kisses him.*

*He resists for a second, but then kisses her back.*

*He kisses her cheek and her neck and her ear.*

ANI. Please.

*He slides down and looks as if he's about to go down on her
when she starts reaching for her phone.*

*He reaches for her hand, interlacing their fingers to stop her.*

LIAM. Tell me what you want.

ANI. I want to watch.

*He kisses her.*

LIAM. You can watch me.

*She giggles.*

*He kisses her more roughly, maybe pins her arms.* ANI *giggles again.*

LIAM *sits back on his heels, defeated, embarrassed.*

ANI. You used to like it.

LIAM. Not this stuff.

ANI. Something else then.

*She kisses him. Strokes his arm.*

Please.

LIAM *sighs. Nods in assent.*

ANI *excitedly grabs the phone.*

*Horrible noises.*

LIAM *winces.*

*She finds another video.*

*She takes his hand and moves it to her. He touches her.*

ANI*'s eyes are glued to her phone.*

LIAM. Look at me.

ANI *looks at him but it's too much for her and she is pulled back to the phone.*

Ani, look at me.

*She doesn't. He goes down on her.*

*Seconds pass. It's clear it's not really working for either of them.*

I hate this.
I can't do this. I can't.

LIAM *sits back.*

I don't know what to do. I actually don't. Can't you see how upset I am?

ANI *reluctantly turns it off. He gets up.*

I can't help you if you don't want to be helped. I don't know – I – I – I –
I don't know what to do. You have some serious intimacy problems and it's too much for me to – I don't know if it's your mum or –

ANI. Ugh come on, Liam, lots of people's mums die!

LIAM. I don't know what to do. I love you so much but this is –

*He seems like he's on the verge of a panic attack or something.*

You won't tell me what's wrong. You won't be vulnerable with me and I –

ANI *holds him, smoothing out his hair. He's crying.*

ANI. Shhh.

LIAM. This is making me so unhappy. I'm sorry I – I –

ANI. I know. I'm sorry.

ANI *sighs.*

*A long pause.* LIAM*'s shallow breath as he cries.*

In Year 9 we had this substitute maths teacher called Mr Franklin. He was only there for like two terms. But he liked me. Probably because I was good at maths but also because I was friendly and kept the top two buttons of my shirt undone. He used to ask me to stay behind after and tell me I was worth way more than the girls I hung out with and when was I going to realise my full potential and that I was so special.

LIAM *looks up at her, concerned.*

It's not as bad as it seems. He fondled me a bit but I just told my head of year and he was gone – I think to another school but I try not to think about that 'cause it makes me…

But I think I want someone to tell me I'm special but it is also so gross to me at the same time. And I think… I think that's what's wrong with me. I've conflated the two. So you – you're so nice and you make me feel so special. But I ruin it because –

LIAM. No, no you don't ruin it – you don't ruin it.

*He holds her face.*

I'm here.

*They kiss.*

*He pulls away, holds her face, looks at her in the eyes…*

Thank you.

*They kiss more passionately, tenderly.*

*She takes his top off.*

*It feels like it may be alright…*

ANI (*between kisses, throwaway*). I can't.

LIAM. What?

ANI. I can't.

ANI *tries to resist but she reaches for her phone.*

LIAM *takes her phone and throws it in one of the water glasses.*


**Eight**

*Kitchen.*

ANI. Do you mind if I work here?

DAD. Course not.

ANI. Don't want to be in my room.

*She waits to see if he clocks what she said, he pretends not to.*

DAD. I've got some fresh peas in the garden. Could use a hand podding them.

ANI. Sure.

DAD. Are you planning on being in tonight?

ANI. I don't know.
Why?

DAD. Just checking.
It's good to have plans. Young women. It's good to go out. Socialise.

*ANI is looking at her bedroom… Is there light coming from her door? Or a noise?*

You didn't stay long at Jasmine's – I thought you'd be gone for a few days at least but –

ANI. Sorry I just.
Can I run through my –

DAD. Oh, Ani, you know I don't know anything about that.

ANI. No I know I just – I want to run through it in front of somebody.

DAD. I thought you said it was just an extract from your book.

ANI. No this is a lecture. For the first years.

DAD. So maybe I'll understand it then?

ANI. No, that's not what I meant.

DAD. I just got in.

ANI. Some light entertainment?

DAD. Oof.

ANI. Please.

DAD. I've had a long day – been at the Crawley's plot since dawn –

ANI. Milton loved gardening!

*DAD grunts, uninterested.*

Come on, a nice thing to do for your daughter.

DAD. I do lots of nice things for you.

ANI. Milton dictated his work to his daughters…

DAD. Yes well he was blind, wasn't he?

ANI. I'm really trying not to be in my room.

*They look at each other.*

DAD. Go on then.

ANI. Are you sure?

DAD. Yeah, go on though before I change my mind.

ANI *stands and grabs her notes, grabs a few things – fusses.*

Come on.

ANI *clears her throat.*

ANI. Forget it.

DAD. What did I do?

ANI. Nothing.

DAD. Come on, why don't you go out for drinks tonight?

ANI. What?

DAD. Take a shower. Get out the house. I'll give you some money.

ANI. What's going on?

DAD. Nothing! I'm just trying to get you up and about a bit! Stop you rotting.

ANI. I'm not a plant.

DAD. Don't you want to –

ANI. Tell me.

DAD. Tell you what?

ANI. Why do you want me out of the house so bad?

DAD. I don't!

*She looks at him.*

ANI. Were you planning on having someone round?

*…He was.*

Who?

DAD. A friend. Just for dinner.
I – just for dinner.

ANI. Don't let me stop you.

DAD. It's okay. I'll rearrange.

ANI. I'll keep out of your way. You can fuck her right out there on the table if you want. I'll keep my headphones in.

DAD. Don't be stupid.

…

ANI (*snapping*). Are we going to do something at the end of the month then?

DAD. What – oh, if you like.

ANI. Would you like to do something?

DAD. If you would, yes, we can do something.

ANI. But you would rather not?

DAD. I didn't say that.

…

ANI. What should we do?

DAD. We can go visit the ashes? Say hello.

ANI. Okay.

DAD. Or we can call Auntie Sha. Go for a meal.

ANI. Do you have any more pictures of her?

DAD. I don't think so. None that you haven't seen.

ANI. Okay.

DAD. Why you asking?

ANI *shrugs*.

I'll cancel tonight.

ANI. I'll go out. It's fine.

DAD. No, it's fine.

ANI. No, I'll go. I'll have a quick shower then I'll call Jasmine or something, see if I can get dinner with her.

…

DAD. Thank you.

ANI. I should get out anyway, you're right.

DAD. Thank you.
I'll introduce you soon. I just –

ANI. I get it. Don't worry.

*He smiles at her and plants a kiss on her head.*

DAD. Okay. I better get to those peas.

*He goes to leave.*

*She wells up.*

ANI. Dad…

DAD. Hey, what? What is it, love?

*He hugs her.*

ANI. I'm sorry.

DAD. What you sorry for?
Love? What you sorry for?

ANI. I – it's quite bad.

DAD. What is?

*He realises.*

*He lets go of her.*

ANI. Dad?

DAD *sighs, exasperated.*

Sorry.

DAD. Do we have to do this now, Ani? Right now?

ANI. I know. I'm sorry.

DAD. It's a big day and I'm all –

ANI *wells up, nods.*

ANI. I'm know I'm just. I'm really sore.

DAD *grimaces, gestures for her to stop.*

DAD. Okay. You can call the doctor in the morning. I'm. I'm going to – do I have to cancel now?

## Nine

*Doctor's consultation room.*

DOCTOR. Anisha Sandhu?

*It's a woman.*

ANI. Ani's fine.

DOCTOR. Sorry about the wait. I'm Dr Chapman. Can I just get your date of birth?

ANI. Yeah twenty-six – oh-one –

DOCTOR. Okay that's all. Fine. So what brings you in today?

ANI. I have some sensitivity in my vagina. Vulva.

DOCTOR. Sensitivity? Okay. Any strong odours?

ANI. No.

DOCTOR. Abnormal discharge?

ANI. Not that I – no. The opposite, really.

DOCTOR. And when did this all start?

ANI. When did what all start?

*Checking her watch.*

DOCTOR. The sensitivity.

ANI. About three weeks ago.

DOCTOR. And have there been any particular changes to your lifestyle in the past three weeks, including sleep pattern and or diet?

ANI. Yes?

DOCTOR. And can you describe those changes for me?

ANI. Well. I'm not sleeping much.

DOCTOR. Are you prone to UTIs and or thrush?

ANI. Yes I guess I am a little – prone? – to them.

DOCTOR. Okay I'm just looking here and it says you've had bacterial vaginosis quite a few times too.

ANI. Yes.

DOCTOR. And there is a family history of cervical cancer, yes?

ANI. Yes. My mother. Grandmother.

DOCTOR. But you get regular screenings, yeah?

ANI. Yes.

DOCTOR. How often?

ANI. Doesn't it say on there?

DOCTOR *stops and looks at* ANI *for the first time.*

DOCTOR. Any irritability?

ANI. …Yes

DOCTOR. Any suicidal thoughts or feeling very low?

ANI. No more than usual.

DOCTOR. Okay, Ani. I'm going to ask you to take off your underwear and lie down here for me. There's a paper sheet if you would like to cover yourself.

ANI. Okay thank you.

DOCTOR. I'll be back shortly. Oh sorry –

ANI *looks at her.*

Would you like a chaperone?

ANI. I –

DOCTOR. Another member of staff present to oversee the observation.

ANI. No, no that's okay.

DOCTOR. Your choice.

DOCTOR *leaves.* ANI *undresses and lies down, covering herself with the paper.*

*She slowly reaches down to her vulva. She winces in pain.*

DOCTOR *knocks and re-enters.* ANI *jumps and withdraws her hand. The* DOCTOR *catches the movement. They look at each other.*

All okay?

ANI. Yep.

DOCTOR. Okay. Let's take a look then.

DOCTOR *lifts up the paper sheet. Looks at her vulva.*

DOCTOR *switches the overhead light on and pulls it closer.*

ANI *flinches.*

ANI. That's bright.

*The* DOCTOR *bends down. Her face is way too close to her thighs.* ANI *freezes.*

DOCTOR. So what I'm seeing here is that you are a disgusting little pervert. And what you deserve is to have all that violence you love to get off on be reenacted on you so you can see – no *feel* – what it's really like.

ANI *looks at the* DOCTOR, *who climbs up on the examination bed in a sexually threatening way.*

*Suddenly the overhead light switches off and the doctor's office goes pitch black.*

*When the lights come back on,* ANI *has the sheet over her and the* DOCTOR *has just entered the room and is shutting the door behind her.*

All okay?

*Nope.*

ANI. ... Yep.

DOCTOR. Okay. Let's take a look then.

DOCTOR *lifts up the paper sheet. Looks at her vulva.*

*She winces.*

Goodness me!
Yes, you're very inflamed.

DOCTOR *switches the overhead light on and pulls it closer.*

ANI *flinches.*

ANI. That's bright.

DOCTOR. All done.

DOCTOR *switches the light off and covers* ANI *back up with the paper.*

So it looks as if you have a bacterial infection. I'm going to prescribe you a short course of antibiotics along with a cream to help soothe the external labia.

ANI. Okay – thank you.

DOCTOR. And I'll have you come back in after you complete the course because there is some broken skin on the clitoris that I am slightly concerned about.

ANI. Okay.

DOCTOR. Now we're going to want to abstain from any sexual activity until you finish the course to prevent further infection.

ANI (*playfully*). Is that like when doctors say don't take alcohol with penicillin though?

DOCTOR. You shouldn't take alcohol with penicillin.

ANI. Oh. Yeah. Of course.

DOCTOR. Will that be an issue?

ANI. No I'm not a big drinker.

DOCTOR. Abstaining from sexual activity?

ANI. Oh – no it'll be fine.

DOCTOR. This is a safe space –

*She looks to the screen to find Ani's name.*

– Anisha.

ANI. Ani's fine.

DOCTOR. You can say whatever you need to in here.

ANI. Okay.

DOCTOR. Does your partner ever become violent during sex?

ANI *laughs.*

DOCTOR *frowns.*

ANI. No! No.

DOCTOR. Okay.

*She frowns. Puzzled.*

ANI. What about masturbation?

DOCTOR. What about masturbation?

ANI. You guys probably know that when we say we drink six units a week we mean six units a day right?

DOCTOR. Do you masturbate six times a day?

ANI. No.

...

Would that be bad?

DOCTOR. The severity of your infection concerns me.
You must be in a lot of pain.

*They make proper eye contact for the first time.*

Do you think you'll be able to refrain from masturbation, Abi?

ANI. Ani.

DOCTOR. Ani, my apologies, do you think you'll be able to refrain from masturbation?

…

ANI. Sure. Of course.

DOCTOR. Great.
Is there anything else I can help you with today?


**Ten**

*The coffee and snack table at a Porn Masturbation Orgasm (PMO) anonymous meeting.*

JAMES. What did you think of the meeting?

ANI. It was okay.

JAMES. First one?

ANI *nods.*

Yeah, I could tell. You were very quiet.

…

I like your shoes.

JAMES *reaches for a doughnut.*

I am going to treat myself to another. I just passed my two-hundred days.

ANI. Congratulations.

JAMES. Yeah and I just got awarded salesman of the month as well. It comes with a big bonus, so pretty pleased with myself.

ANI. Well done.

JAMES. Yeah big bonus.

ANI. Where do you work?

JAMES. Mercedes.

ANI. That's cool.

JAMES. What do you do?

ANI. I'm a... teacher?

JAMES. I'm glad you weren't my teacher. Wouldn't have been able to concentrate.

...

What was your name again?

ANI. Ani.

*They don't shake hands.*

I read online that it takes forty days to rewire your brain.

JAMES. How long has it been?

ANI. Like, four hours.

*He smiles.*

JAMES. That's not true. About the rewiring.

ANI. Oh.

*She readjusts herself and flinches in pain.*

JAMES. How are you feeling?

ANI. Like shit.

JAMES. You got cuts? Rashes?

*ANI nods.*

Alright so right now: you're a puppet. You're not in control of yourself. Body or mind.

ANI. Yeah, it certainly feels like that.

JAMES. But you made it here. So that's something. Well done.

ANI. Thanks.

JAMES. Now one of the most valuable things, I find, is to remember that you're never too smart for an addiction.

*It's good advice.*

And because I'm a smart guy, it took me a while to admit to myself I was weak enough to succumb to an addiction.

ANI. Yes you seem very smart.

JAMES. Especially a Porn, Masturbation, Orgasm addiction.

ANI. Yes, doesn't carry the cadence of heroin or alcohol does it?

JAMES. I've refrained from porn and masturbation for over two hundred days now.

ANI. Yes, congratulations.

JAMES. Watching the way your ass was sat on that stool during the meeting made me want to go to the bathroom and fap one out though.

*ANI shifts on her feet uncomfortably.*

ANI. When did you start watching?

JAMES. Since I was ten. You?

ANI. Same yeah. Eleven, twelve.

JAMES. So you're into the dark shit by now yeah?

*ANI looks at her feet and nods.*

What's your thing?

ANI. I mean I don't know if I feel comfortable –

JAMES. Mine was snuff. Unconscious. As long as they weren't moving my dick was as hard as a gear stick stuck in reverse.

*He laughs.*

God it made me feel terrible about myself. And I come from a religious family so you can imagine.

ANI *looks at her feet and nods. He looks at her feet too.*

I bet yours is like those kidnap ones. Where the girls get the shit beaten out of them.

ANI. Why would you think that?

JAMES. Alright. Calm down. I'm just trying to help.

ANI *inhales.*

So what did you make of it? Actually?

ANI. The session?

JAMES. Yeah

ANI. Lots of men talking about how their dads hit them.

JAMES. Surprising?

ANI. Yeah. I didn't know it was so common for people like this.

JAMES. Ah yeah.
What's your dad like?

ANI. Fine.

JAMES. You sure?

ANI. Yeah.

JAMES. Mum?

ANI. She's dead.

JAMES. What she die of?

ANI. Cervical cancer. When I was fourteen.

JAMES. There you go.

ANI. What?

JAMES. Same thing, isn't it.

ANI (*laughing, despite herself*). No?

JAMES. Addicts – especially porn and sex addicts – have trouble with seeing women as real people. Obviously you've got your regular old psychos who were just dropped on their heads as babies, but a lot of us it's cause they had to grow up wanting to save their mums – from beatings, drugs, whatever – breast cancer –

ANI. Cervical

JAMES. Yeah so we can only really relate to women as objects. We have to, like, disconnect? 'Cause if they're real then –

ANI. Then you can't fuck them.

JAMES. – then it's too vulnerable. Women must be – what's the word? Animalous? objects –

ANI. Anonymous?

JAMES. That's it. And even better if they're 2D, right? So you don't have to worry about them.

ANI. Oh.

JAMES. You don't have to save them. Even though it was never really in our power to save them in the first place. My dad was a tank.

ANI *blinks at him.*

But it *is* in your power to stop beating one out.

ANI (*laughing*). Don't say beating one out.

JAMES. Apologies. We aren't used to ladies around here.

ANI. So is that supposed to solve it?

JAMES. You wish! It's just to help you think a bit – like maybe these urges aren't me, maybe they're about something else.

ANI. So what do I do?

JAMES. Well. You have two options. You can be a slave or you can be a warrior.

ANI. Excuse me?

JAMES. You can be a slave to your addiction. You can let it ruin your relationships, your life.

ANI (*jokingly*). Too late.

JAMES. Or you can be a warrior and rise above. Put on your armour and slay the darkness inside of you. Tell the urges to get *fucked.*

ANI. Right.

JAMES. It is called the warrior because you are in a fight, and the enemy is yourself. And your past.

ANI. No yeah I get that

JAMES. It's the manly option – to overcome hardship and triumph with power –

ANI. The manly option.

JAMES. Don't get upset about it. It just means it will probably be even harder for you, you know, as a –

*He gestures to her breasts.*

ANI. Don't do that.

JAMES. Why not?

ANI. Because it makes me feel uncomfortable.

JAMES. Think about what you watch.

ANI. That's different.

JAMES. Look, Ans, can I call you Ans? I can help you. Do you want my help?

ANI. Yes.

*He rests a hand on her arm. She stares at it.*

JAMES. You need to say it. You need to admit that you need help.

ANI. I need help.

*It shifts.*

JAMES. Beg me.

ANI. I need help.

JAMES. Yes.

ANI. I need help. I'll do anything.

*He removes his hand from her arm and tugs at the fabric around his crotch.*

JAMES. I bet you will you, you desperate slut.

ANI. Yes. I'm so sore, Daddy. Can you help me?

*It shifts back, but* ANI *is slow to catch up.*

Please, Daddy.

JAMES. You what?

ANI *refocuses.*

ANI. I need help, please. I came here to get help.

JAMES *looks at her… sadly?*

JAMES. It's been ages since I touched a girl in real life.

ANI *laughs uncomfortably.*

Can I… just…

*He reaches out and gently touches her cheek.*

*She looks at him in the eyes.*

ANI. Are you okay?

JAMES (*panicked*). I can't feel anything.

*He removes his hand and readjusts his suit.*

You were the first girl to ever come to one of these meetings. You're one of a kind.

ANI. Lucky me.

JAMES. But hey listen, the guys wanted me to tell you that they think it's best if you find another group. You're a trigger, for sure.

## Eleven

*An event room.*

ANI *stands alone. An* OLD MAN *approaches her and taps his glass rhythmically.*

OLD MAN. Excuse me, can you top me up? I don't know where you are all hiding away. I can't find you anywhere.

ANI. What?

OLD MAN. I've *guzzled* this glass down –

ANI. Oh, no, sorry – I'm – I'm not a waiter – I'm – I – this is for me.

OLD MAN. What's that?

ANI (*louder*). I am the recipient of the –

*A* WOMAN, *older than* ANI, *glides towards her.*

WOMAN. Ani. Congratulations!

*She kisses her on the cheek.*

I see you've met Giles. He loved your book.

OLD MAN. Who?

WOMAN. Giles, this is Ani Sandhu. SHE WON THE AWARD.

OLD MAN. You? You're very young.

WOMAN. Isn't she? The youngest woman ever –

ANI. Person. Thank you.

WOMAN. You look so fuckable as well, darling! Doesn't she? Hardly seems fair!

*They laugh.*

OLD MAN. Sandhu is an interesting name, where's that from?

ANI. Will you excuse me I –

ANI *turns away and collides with* SAM.

ANI. Sorry!

SAM. No, that was my bad. Sorry.

WOMAN. Did you know Lensk is here?

OLD MAN. Lensk is here!

*They leave.*

SAM *offers a hand to shake.*

SAM. I'm Sam. Sam Lister. Big fan. Loved the book. Well deserved. Really well deserved.

ANI. Thank you. Are you a – sorry – what brings you here?

SAM. I'm about to start my masters under Birkman.

ANI. Oh great. He's great. You'll have a great time –

OLD MAN. Excuse me, can you top me up?

ANI. Have you seen him actually? I don't want to start without him –

SAM. Yeah it's going really well actually. I'm just trying to figure out the right angle – the right position –

ANI. Sure. Well that will all reveal itself with –

SAM. Doggy.

ANI. What?

SAM. The right dogma, you know. I know it'll come in my face but while you're in the trenches it's a bit of a bitch.

ANI *laughs, a bit uncomfortable.*

Look at you, are you feeling a bit overwhelmed?

*He touches her arm.* ANI *looks at it.*

ANI. I'm fine.

SAM. I actually went to your lecture series at the UFV when I was doing my A Levels.

ANI. Oh you went to those did you? I'm honoured.

SAM. I'm just very big. A very big and hard fan.

ANI. Good luck with it all. I'm just going to prep my –

SAM. Sorry if this is – but would you be down for getting a coffee sometime? I'd love to lick your pussy about my thesis.

ANI. Uhmm – I…

Birkman will give you my email.

SAM. Why –

ANI. Do you know if he's here yet?

SAM. Who?

ANI. Birkman!

SAM. Um yeah I think I saw him –

*WOMAN and* OLD MAN *reappear suddenly.*

WOMAN. Wait! Tell us what's next!

SAM. I'll email you –

*He leaves.*

OLD MAN. It's a good chunk of ass – you can take three years off to write and live like a queen.

ANI. I think I'll stay teaching, I like teaching.

WOMAN. God why!?

OLD MAN. What's the second book?

ANI. I actually don't know yet –

WOMAN. Nor do you need to! The world is your oyster!

*She slaps* ANI *on the bum.*

ANI. Have you seen Birkman?

WOMAN. No. I don't know how you do it – spend all your time giving head –

ANI. Excuse me?

WOMAN. – *in* the head – of that vile old man Milton. But yes she's bloody brilliant.

You'll see –

ANI. Okay bye!

WOMAN. No no no. You have to go insert your award now! Up your little fanny.

OLD MAN. I look forward to seeing you on your knees while I choke you so much you can't even breathe, let alone beg me to stop. And when you finally pass out I'll piss in your mouth, my dear.

ANI. I just need to –

WOMAN. Please – for after.

*She ushers* ANI *up.*

It is my absolute *pleasure* to present this award – from the Royal Fellowship Society Foundation Trust –  to the begging, the gagging, the wet… Ani Sandhu!

*She hands the award to* ANI.

ANI. Hello. Hi. This is an incredible honour. And to see so many respected academics here – wow. Thank you.

I never thought I would end up here when I first encountered Milton's work as an undergraduate. I never thought my adolescent outrage over the misogyny of this canonical writer would flourish into a great passion and appreciation.

*She laughs sadly.*

There are so many people I'd like to thank – and I'll get to that but – um – I've been thinking a lot about –

What have I been thinking a lot about?

*She laughs nervously.*

I'm actually thinking about giving into temptation. The original sin.

The temptation scene in Genesis is less than ten lines long. Milton takes a lot longer. Most of Book Nine. And it's boring. We know she's going to eat it. She's jealous of Adam and God being in their boys group. She's having an identity crisis and wants to understand who she is. All of that.

But I feel like we forget that it's really about her lust. She's seduced by this juicy erect penis of a snake telling her she's beautiful.

*Some titters of uncomfortableness throughout her audience.*

She has a pull to be submissive. After all, that's all she knows. She's made from a rib for god's sake. She can't fight it anymore, her lust is too overpowering. It's *in* her – rotting away in her. She really wants it. She really wants to just go home, prop her laptop on her chest and find one of her favourite videos, buried on the seventh page.

*She squeezes her legs together like she's trying to stop herself orgasming.*

It would be about nine minutes long, but she'd finish in four.

So of course Eve eats the forbidden fruit. Even though she knows she's going to be punished. Even though she knows it will bring her great shame…

*She sounds like she's going to continue but –*

## Twelve

*Ani's childhood bedroom.*

*ANI, in bed, is watching porn and trying to masturbate but it's painful for her. She is comatose, apart from occasional flinches of pain and bursts of frustration.*

*Her DAD knocks and enters. He's been working himself up for this.*

*ANI shuts her laptop quickly – not as quickly as she did before. They look at each other.*

DAD. Hi

ANI. Hi

   …

Can you go away please I'm not hungry.

…

DAD. Do you want to give me your laptop?

ANI *becomes on alert.*

ANI. Why?

DAD. Ani…

DAD *leans down to take the laptop but* ANI *cradles it.*

ANI. No, I need it for work.

DAD. What work? You're not – you've not been working for weeks. They keep calling you –

ANI. How the fuck would you know?

DAD. Liam said –

ANI. Liam can fuck off. So can you.

*He doesn't move.*

Fuck off, Dad!

DAD (*wincing at the language*). Ani, don't speak to me like that.

…

Give me the laptop, please.

DAD *tries to grab the laptop again but* ANI *scurries away from him, wrapped in her sheets.*

ANI. NO!

DAD. Please, love – I can see it's – it's gotten bad again.

ANI. No it hasn't.

DAD. Come on. The laptop.

ANI. I just need to manage it a bit better but I'm fine.

DAD. That's not what you do with these things.

ANI. I'm fine! I'm not your pisshead mum, I'm fine.

DAD *goes in a bit more forcefully and manages to get a hand on her laptop.* ANI *panics –*

LEAVE ME ALONE

DAD. I can't.

ANI. I'm going to end up doing it so you might as well let me do it in the house –

DAD. No, love. I'm sorry

*He climbs into bed with her and gets the laptop.*

ANI. Get off of me!

*He quickly climbs out, clinging on to the laptop and backing towards the door.*

No please. Please don't. Please. I'm sorry.

Dad?

Dad, I'm sorry.

*Trying a new tack, she crawls over to him. She tries to hug him but he winces away from her, protecting the laptop.*

DAD. Stop.

*His shame and disgust upsets her.*

*At their new distance it seems to be an exhausted stalemate.*

*But suddenly Ani's phone beeps.*

*It's somewhere in the tangle of her bedsheets.*

*Her face lights up and she dives for it, her* DAD *does too.*

ANI *finds it first, but* DAD *grabs her wrist and pries it out of her hands.*

*Once he lets go,* ANI *screams and attacks her* DAD, *wrestling him. They struggle for what seems like hours.*

ANI *bites her* DAD. *He gasps in pain and releases the phone.*

ANI *runs out with her phone.*

DAD *tries to get up. He looks very old.*

**Thirteen**

*A bedroom. Maybe in darkness.*

SAM. My roommates are out. So.
    We just moved in. Sorry for the boxes.

ANI. Do you want to kiss me?

SAM. Yeah?

> *They kiss clumsily.*

> ANI *starts undressing.*

> Whoa. This is. Okay.

> SAM *starts undressing.*

> *They kiss more.*

ANI. Are you excited?

SAM. Yes

ANI. What are you excited to do to me?

SAM. Umm. Fuck you?

> ANI *sticks her hand down her trousers then removes it instantly.*

ANI. Touch me.

> SAM *puts his hand down* ANI*'s underwear.*

> *He fiddles around a bit.*

SAM. That good?

> ANI*'s hand drifts to her vagina but she stops herself.*

ANI. Can you tie my hands behind my back?

SAM. Seriously?

ANI. Yes.

SAM. Okay – um – what should I use?

ANI. Your belt?

SAM. Really? Okay yeah.

   SAM *whips off his belt and ties it around* ANI*'s hands.*

ANI. Tighter please.

SAM. Okay.

   *He double knots it.*

   ANI *tries to get out but can't.*

ANI. Okay.

   ANI *gets down on her knees.*

SAM. Fuck.

ANI. Do you have a tie?

SAM. Um – yes – is the belt not tight enough?

ANI. No. Can you. Can you blindfold me?
   Is that okay?

SAM. Yes!

   SAM *scrambles up and grabs a tie. He ties it around her eyes.*

   This is so hot.

ANI. Yeah.

   *He steps back to look at her. She doesn't know where he is.*

   You okay?

SAM. Yes!

   *Beat.*

   Can I –

ANI. Do what you want.

SAM. Shit.
   This is so fucking hot.

   *He reaches out and slips a finger in her mouth.*

   You're my teacher

ANI. Wait. We need a safeword.

SAM. Okay.

ANI. Something un sexy.

SAM. What about
    Milton?

    ANI *laughs sadly.*

    No?

ANI. Yeah no sure.

SAM. Cool. What do you want me to do now?

ANI. I want you to do what you want.

SAM. Okay…

    *He bends down and kisses her sloppily.* ANI *pulls away.*

ANI. Do you want me?

SAM. Yes!

ANI. What do you want about me?

SAM. Umm I want – all of you?

ANI. What do you want to do to me?

SAM. Umm – I want to fuck you.

ANI. How badly?

SAM. Badly.

ANI. What if I don't want you to?

SAM. What?

ANI. You're my student and I gave you a bad grade and now
    you want to punish me.

SAM. But we don't get grades for lectures?

ANI. Pretend. Just whatever, pretend you're mad at me.

    SAM *apprehensively puts one hand around* ANI*'s throat.*

SAM. You like that?

    ANI *nods.*

ANI. More.

> SAM *slips two fingers into* ANI*'s mouth.*

SAM. God you're fucking nasty.

> *He moves the fingers in and out of her mouth, falling into a trance.*
>
> *He grabs her hair.*
>
> *He pulls it back.*
>
> ANI*'s neck at an uncomfortable angle.*
>
> ANI *eeks in pain a bit.*
>
> I said do you like that?

ANI. Yes.

SAM. Yes what?

> ANI *laughs.*

ANI. Do you want me to call you sir?

> SAM *pulls her hair back more.*

SAM. Don't laugh at me.

ANI. Okay.

SAM. Stupid bitch.

> *He slaps her.*
>
> You like that don't you?
>
> *He hits her harder.*
>
> SAM *puts his hand over her face, over her mouth and eyes.*
>
> Shut up.
>
> You're a slut. Asking for this.
> My teacher is a slut.
>
> *He chokes her while he shimmies out of his trousers.*
>
> You love it don't you?

ANI (*almost inaudible*). Milton.

SAM. Open your mouth

SAM *prises her mouth open.*

SAM *spits in it.*

ANI *retches and spits on the floor.*

ANI. What the fuck –

SAM. Yeah you like that don't you, you whore. You like to be punished.

*He slaps her again.*

ANI. Milton.

*He suddenly comes to and takes a step backwards. Looking disgusted with himself.*

I can't see.
I can't see.


## Fourteen

*An office.*

ANI *looks at her advisor,* BIRKMAN. *Why is it her dad?*

ANI. Hi.

BIRKMAN. Ani.

BIRKMAN *stands. A hug feels like a possibility but they don't.*

ANI. I bought some chocolates. For you and Jules. To say sorry. I'm sorry.

BIRKMAN. That is very nice of you, Ani. I'll pass that along.

ANI. Good.

BIRKMAN. Uh. Why don't you take a seat –

ANI. How is she?

BIRKMAN. Well, thank you. She's been sad to hear what's going on. With you. As have I.

ANI. Yes.

…

BIRKMAN. Well? How are you?

ANI *just shakes her head. She doesn't know.*

BIRKMAN *sighs, exasperated.*

I haven't heard from you in weeks. Even an email would have been – we've all been very worried.

ANI *hangs her head like a child being told off.*

What on earth happened?

ANI. I don't know what happened. If I knew what had happened it wouldn't have happened.

BIRKMAN. Not a flawless logic there, I'm afraid.

ANI (*trying her luck*). You hate a tautology.

BIRKMAN. Popeian doggerel! Yes, you know me well.

*He pulls his chair closer to him and gestures for her to sit.*

ANI *smiles at him and sits down. He smiles back sadly.*

Why haven't you been to see me? I would have hoped that – whatever it was – you could have – uh –

ANI. I was embarrassed. I let everyone down.

BIRKMAN. No. No.

ANI. I'm so sorry to let you down.

BIRKMAN *looks at her. It feels as if he should put a hand on her leg but he doesn't.*

BIRKMAN. Ani, you should know that teaching you – watching you grow – I should say *out*grow – has been one of – if not *the* highlight of my career –

ANI (*moved*). Oh.

BIRKMAN. And I can assure you I have been fighting tooth and nail for you to keep your job but I can't do it without your participation –

ANI. What?

BIRKMAN. The board is very –

ANI. Have I lost my job?

BIRKMAN *blinks at her.*

BIRKMAN. I assumed – because you're here – you would have read my –

ANI. No no no please I can't lose my job. I need to be working right now.

BIRKMAN. Ani there were many, many complaints.

ANI. About the – your masters student?

BIRKMAN. What masters student? The board doesn't want you interacting with students. So we can't have you get back to – uh – teaching just yet.

ANI. No. No I can't – I need – surely there is some – I can get a – surely PhD students are okay? I can oversee thesis prep? I can –

BIRKMAN. Ani, listen. The university has access to some decent counselling facilities. Shall I give you their contact information?

ANI. I don't want counselling! I want to get back to work. Please. What do I need to do?

BIRKMAN. Why don't you start with some counselling? Maybe we can get a doctor's note. That way it can be viewed as a suspension –

ANI. Fuck, is it more than a suspension?

BIRKMAN. Language.

ANI. Sorry. But – is it – it's more than – is it final? Have I –

BIRKMAN. Well, let's – the board are pretty fixed – but – there were –

ANI. Okay fine – but – we can start talking about the second
book? Yes? I have some ideas –

*She rustles in her pockets with scraps of paper.*

BIRKMAN. Well, it's part of a – uh – longer discussion. We've
all been quite – uh – concerned.

ANI. I'm fine now. Honestly. I'm ready to get back on track.
Second book. Where are my fu– notes?

*She is emptying the contents of her pockets trying
desperately to find the right scrap of paper.*

BIRKMAN. Ani.

*He puts a hand on her hand to stop her rustling.*

The extremity of your – uh – incident – means we can't just
dive straight back into it, I'm afraid.

ANI. Why not? I won't do it again. I swear.

BIRKMAN. Well, let's just put a pin in that for the meantime…

ANI. Why?

BIRKMAN *doesn't want to break it to her.*

Did they – do I have to give my award back?

BIRKMAN *can't say it, but* ANI *understands. She starts
crying.*

BIRKMAN. Goodness. Okay. Well, there's no need for that. It's
just Milton.

*She cries harder at that.*

*He grabs a box of tissues and offers them to her. She takes
one.*

BIRKMAN *looks uncomfortable but patiently waits.*

*She steadies herself.*

ANI. What do I need to do?

BIRKMAN. Well – I don't want to – uh – force you into
anything you're not ready to do.

ANI. I'll do anything!

BIRKMAN. Why don't we start with counselling? I'll get their
number for you –

*He turns around to look at the number in his office.*

It's bloody stuffy in here, isn't it? Aren't you hot?

BIRKMAN *takes his blazer off and loosens his tie.*

ANI. Oh. Okay. Yes.

*ANI reluctantly takes her jumper/jacket off.*

BIRKMAN. That's better. Alright. I really think you should
check in with this counsellor, just for a few weeks – my
niece had a spot of bother with her – uh – eating and she
found counselling very – uh – helpful!
So. Here it is!

BIRKMAN *turns around with the counsellor's info –*

ANI. I'll do anything.

BIRKMAN. Glad to hear it.

*They stare at each other.*

ANI. Oh. Okay.

*ANI methodically undoes her shirt buttons and slides off her
chair onto her knees.*

BIRKMAN. Ani? What are you doing?

ANI . No, it's okay. I understand.

BIRKMAN. Why are you –

ANI. I'm sorry – did you want to do that?

*She sticks her chest out as if preparing for* BIRKMAN *to
undress her.*

BIRKMAN. Ani, stop that.

ANI. I want to – I swear. Please go ahead.

BIRKMAN. Get up!

*She crawls over to him and begins unzipping his flies.*

ANI. I want to. Really. I want it in my mouth.

BIRKMAN. Oh my god.

> BIRKMAN *stands up and grabs her wrists to stop her from touching his penis.*

ANI. I'll do anything. Wherever you like.

> BIRKMAN *looks down at* ANI, *shocked and scared.*

> *For a second, maybe his face flashes with the tantalising possibility of this exchange –*

> *But then he decides against it and yanks* ANI *up on her feet.*

BIRKMAN. Get up – stop!

ANI. I just want to get back to work.

BIRKMAN. Ani, what do you think is going on here?

> ANI *blinks.*

> I am not asking you to do anything – uh – sexual! Is that clear?

> ANI *nods.*

> Is that clear?

ANI. Yes.

> …

> I'm sorry.

> BIRKMAN *gestures that it's alright… but he opens the door.*

BIRKMAN. I hope you know I would never – what's wrong with you?

> ANI *thinks. She doesn't know. She thinks about that student, Bex. Maybe she was right.*

> *She starts crying again.*

> BIRKMAN *sighs in quiet frustration and grabs the box of tissues again, offering them to her.*

> *She takes one.*

**Fifteen**

ANI. I think the second book would have been on this Milton
poem called *Lycidas*. Don't know if there would have been
enough there to be honest – for a whole book – it's only
two hundred lines but… yeah. It's dedicated to his friend
who died. He drowned at sea. And I always liked how the
irregular rhymes are sort of like a choppy ocean. And I think
maybe that's why it's not very well known – it's hard to
write about because you can't quite put your feet on the
bottom of it. It keeps moving around you a bit unpredictably.

But if I'm being honest the poem is just really sad, and it
captures the weirdness of grief really well. And it felt oddly
relevant to me. It starts with all these inversions. Picking
blackberries becomes this violent act, someone too young
dies. And that person was the best singer so who is supposed
to sing at his funeral?

Um. So it's typical with this often really stuffy genre of
'pastoral elegy' to compare your dead friend or lover or
family member to a figure from Antiquity. And Milton
compares his dead friend to this hero called Lycidas. And
Lycidas was this politician – in history or mythology or
however you like to look at it – who suggested a compromise
in the Greco-Persian war. And you can see this in the poem –
it's all about compromise. The compromise of war, the
compromise of grief.

What's funny – or terrible – was that Lycidas was stoned to
death for his suggestion. And the women on the island ran to
his home and stoned his wife and children. I like when those
anecdotes don't let you forget about the brutality of women.

I feel brutal when I watch those women's faces change. And
you can tell they are just enduring it now. Or when they
push against the man to get him to ease up or stop but he
just grabs their wrist and puts it somewhere else. I feel brutal
when I cum to that, yeah.

The poem also has all these things about nature, about how the woods are sad Lycidas is dead, how the willows weep. Milton describes jasmines that are too pale, the pansy freaked with jet. I always think about my dad when I read that, or I think about that when I'm thinking of my dad outside with his plants. How when he was overwhelmed with her vomiting and her bleeding he would go outside and tend to his garden.

I've never spoken to him about it but I suppose he liked that things keep growing, that nature is indifferent. I remember writing about that when I was twenty and my teacher's red line through it. He scribbled YES, SO? next to it. I found that funny because that was the point, that was the fucking point. The sheer rage that everyone moves on and everything keeps growing and moving. And that Milton created a world where nothing was indifferent, where everything and everyone was as affected as him. Where the seasons literally stopped because his grief was so painful.

The poem starts with the phrase – Yet Once More. I like that. It's like 'here we go again'. But also it's like this is the last time. It's both.

But I should say that not everyone liked this poem. People say it's too learned to be passionate. But I take personal offence at that so. A lot of really esteemed critics argue that it's too full of pleasure to be about the pain of loss. That's like the general 'it's not very good' school of thought.

But god that is so wrong. Because the pleasure covers it up, the pleasure is very necessary.

Because who wants just pain? That would be...

ANI *fidgets, takes a deep breath.*

*She takes her phone out. Types something. Is she going to masturbate?*

*She puts the phone down.*

He's obsessed with that, Milton. The pain and the pleasure sitting together. You don't just run from one to get to the other – they are –

*She gestures that they're connected.*

Like the tree that Eve eats from – the tree has the knowledge of good AND evil. You can't have one without the other. *Yet once more.*

And it takes you somewhere else.

To a totally different world.

An Eden.

Full of flowers and violence and pain and pleasure.

And the thought of stepping out of that –

*Suddenly she snatches her phone up.*

*She turns the volume up just a little.*

*She masturbates.*

*She hears footsteps.*

*Her DAD enters.*

*He clocks what she's doing.*

*She keeps masturbating.*

DAD *takes a few steps forward.*

*He turns away.*

*Eventually –*

DAD. Where have you been?

ANI. Out.

DAD *nods.*

DAD. I was worried.

ANI. Well, I'm home now so.

*Beat.*

DAD. Ani maybe you stop that?

ANI (*tears in her voice*). It's today.

DAD. It is today, yes.

ANI *shakes her head. Her hand keeps moving.*

I was looking at this –

*He has a photo album.*

I thought you might like to see.

*He puts the photo album he is holding onto the table.*

Come on. Sit down with me.

ANI *slowly sits down next to him. Her hand is still down her trousers.*

*He opens the album, angles it towards her. He flicks through a few pages.*

Look at you there! Your hair!

DAD *reaches out to take her hand out from her trousers. She tugs away.*

*He hovers for a moment, unsure of what to do, then returns to the album.*

I loved that mirror in the old house. Hundreds and hundreds of you in all directions. You'd spend hours there when you were little.

…

That's a good photo, isn't it.

…

I loved that jacket. I wonder where that went.

…

Do you remember that trip? Me and you – first time out of the country together!

Don't know who was more excited if I'm honest.

Now where was this? The lake looks like the one near Babaji's place but I know it can't be because – where was it – was it at the Tokay's place?

Was it?

*He looks to* ANI, *sees where her hand still is, then looks away.*

Must have been. That was nice. She taught you how to swim there.

Remember? You loved being in the water but the minute anyone let go of you you'd scream –

ANI. Yeah.

*Maybe she starts crying. Maybe he does. Maybe it's really silent.*

*He flips over a page. Her hand is still.*

DAD. Remember that beautiful yellow dress? You loved whenever she wore it.

Tugged at her and followed her around! I think it's still upstairs if you want it?

ANI *slowly removes her hand and puts it on the photo.*

I'll go get it for you after. That'll be nice.

This was at her summer party. You remember those, don't you? We'd both drunk too much so had to pull over on the way home and have a snooze. You read to us as we dozed off. Do you remember that? How old were you there?

Probably eleven or something. Not very good that, oh dear.

But you loved reading. You loved reading out loud. Remember those readings you did for us? She loved those. Always said you were a better teacher than she was!

*He turns the page again. And again. Maybe those are the funeral pictures. Then –*

There you are on your first day of uni.

ANI. I can't.

DAD. You can't what?
You can't what, Ani?

DAD *inhales shallowly, eyes glued to the table. He keeps going through tears.*

I remember the first time you came back, during Christmas holidays. You could not stop talking about Milton. And there was that one thing you kept talking about – what was it – shit.

…

Ani? What was it?

…

And you came home for the first time since you'd left and I was so pleased to see you. And we were having dinner and you were talking so much that food was flying out your mouth but I didn't want to interrupt you because you seemed so… happy.

But if I remembered it right – this thing – it means like – happy fault? Right? Is that right?

ANI *nods.*

And it's in the very last bit of *Paradise Lost*? I remember cause you got your book out and it didn't take you long to find it because you just flicked to the back. And it's when Adam and Eve are leaving Eden, right? And they are crying because they are sad and really ashamed 'cause they lost their clothes? But they realise it's going to be okay? And don't they hold hands as they leave? Is that right?

You gotta help me out here, Ani.

*She sniffles and nods.*

Well, I'm bad with the details but I think I got the gist. And I remember you being really excited about the line that was – like – it's like the world was all before them? Ahead of them? And I remember thinking – well, I remember thinking jesus is this going to be what our talks are like from now on? – but no, I thought – yeah – I like that. Light out of darkness. Good from bad. The struggle is… the struggle can have good… outcomes. And that made sense to me because when I'm planting, the bulb is in the dark and then it works really hard to get out of there. But when it does, it's really pretty, you know?

This is probably all very obvious to you. I'm sorry. But.
I just wanted to tell you that I think of that a lot when
I'm working. And it makes me think of you. And your
excitement and enthusiasm. And how smart you are.

And I think of you sitting where you are now, bits of food
flying about...

ANI *reaches out with both her hands and takes her* DAD's
*hand in hers. He takes her hands in both of his.*

*End.*

**A Nick Hern Book**

*Porn Play* first published in Great Britain as a paperback original in 2025 by Nick Hern Books Limited, The Glasshouse, 49a Goldhawk Road, London W12 8QP, in association with the Royal Court Theatre, London

*Porn Play* © 2025 Sophia Chetin-Leuner

Sophia Chetin-Leuner has asserted her right to be identified as the author of this work

Cover design by Guy Sanders at Keeper Studio

Designed and typeset by Nick Hern Books, London
Printed in Great Britain by Mimeo Ltd, Huntingdon, Cambridgeshire PE29 6XX

A CIP catalogue record for this book is available from the British Library

ISBN 978 1 83904 476 2

**Amateur Performing Rights**    Applications for performance, including readings and excerpts, by amateurs in the English language throughout the world should be addressed to the Performing Rights Department, Nick Hern Books, The Glasshouse, 49a Goldhawk Road, London W12 8QP, *tel* +44 (0)20 8749 4953, *email* rights@nickhernbooks.co.uk, except as follows:

*Australia:* ORiGiN Theatrical, *email* enquiries@originmusic.com.au, *web* www.origintheatrical.com.au

*New Zealand:* Play Bureau, 20 Rua Street, Mangapapa, Gisborne, 4010, *tel* +64 21 258 3998, *email* info@playbureau.com

*United States of America and Canada:* United Agents, see details below.

**Professional Performing Rights**    Applications for performance by professionals in any medium and any language throughout the world (and amateur and stock performances in the United States of America and Canada) should be addressed to should be addressed to United Agents Ltd, 12–26 Lexington St, London W1F 0LE, *tel* +44 (0)20 3214 0800, *fax* +44 (0)20 3214 0801, *email* info@unitedagents.co.uk

No performance of any kind may be given unless a licence has been obtained. Applications should be made before rehearsals begin. Publication of this play does not necessarily indicate its availability for amateur performance.

**Woodland
CARBON**
www.woodlandcarbon.co.uk
NICK HERN BOOKS
Printed on Carbon Captured paper

www.nickhernbooks.co.uk/environmental-policy

Nick Hern Books' authorised representative in the EU is
Easy Access System Europe – Mustamäe tee 50, 10621 Tallinn, Estonia
*email* gpsr.requests@easproject.com